FREE Test Taking Tips DVD Offer

To help us better serve you, we have developed a Test Taking Tips DVD that we would like to give you for FREE. **This DVD covers world-class test taking tips that you can use to be even more successful when you are taking your test.**

All that we ask is that you email us your feedback about your study guide. Please let us know what you thought about it – whether that is good, bad or indifferent.

To get your **FREE Test Taking Tips DVD**, email freedvd@studyguideteam.com with “FREE DVD” in the subject line and the following information in the body of the email:

a. The title of your study guide.

b. Your product rating on a scale of 1-5, with 5 being the highest rating.

c. Your feedback about the study guide. What did you think of it?

d. Your full name and shipping address to send your free DVD.

If you have any questions or concerns, please don’t hesitate to contact us at freedvd@studyguideteam.com.

Thanks again!

aPHR Study Guide

aPHR Certification Study Guide and Practice Exam Questions for the Associate Professional in Human Resources Exam [2nd Edition]

TPB Publishing

Written and edited by TPB Publishing.

ISBN 13: 9781628458251
ISBN 10: 1628458259

Table of Contents

Quick Overview

As you draw closer to taking your exam, effective preparation becomes more and more important. Thankfully, you have this study guide to help you get ready. Use this guide to help keep your studying on track and refer to it often.

This study guide contains several key sections that will help you be successful on your exam. The guide contains tips for what you should do the night before and the day of the test. Also included are test-taking tips. Knowing the right information is not always enough. Many well-prepared test takers struggle with exams. These tips will help equip you to accurately read, assess, and answer test questions.

A large part of the guide is devoted to showing you what content to expect on the exam and to helping you better understand that content. In this guide are practice test questions so that you can see how well you have grasped the content. Then, answer explanations are provided so that you can understand why you missed certain questions.

Don't try to cram the night before you take your exam. This is not a wise strategy for a few reasons. First, your retention of the information will be low. Your time would be better used by reviewing information you already know rather than trying to learn a lot of new information. Second, you will likely become stressed as you try to gain a large amount of knowledge in a short amount of time. Third, you will be depriving yourself of sleep. So be sure to go to bed at a reasonable time the night before. Being well-rested helps you focus and remain calm.

Be sure to eat a substantial breakfast the morning of the exam. If you are taking the exam in the afternoon, be sure to have a good lunch as well. Being hungry is distracting and can make it difficult to focus. You have hopefully spent lots of time preparing for the exam. Don't let an empty stomach get in the way of success!

When travelling to the testing center, leave earlier than needed. That way, you have a buffer in case you experience any delays. This will help you remain calm and will keep you from missing your appointment time at the testing center.

Be sure to pace yourself during the exam. Don't try to rush through the exam. There is no need to risk performing poorly on the exam just so you can leave the testing center early. Allow yourself to use all of the allotted time if needed.

Remain positive while taking the exam even if you feel like you are performing poorly. Thinking about the content you should have mastered will not help you perform better on the exam.

Once the exam is complete, take some time to relax. Even if you feel that you need to take the exam again, you will be well served by some down time before you begin studying again. It's often easier to convince yourself to study if you know that it will come with a reward!

Test-Taking Strategies

1. Predicting the Answer

When you feel confident in your preparation for a multiple-choice test, try predicting the answer before reading the answer choices. This is especially useful on questions that test objective factual knowledge. By predicting the answer before reading the available choices, you eliminate the possibility that you will be distracted or led astray by an incorrect answer choice. You will feel more confident in your selection if you read the question, predict the answer, and then find your prediction among the answer choices. After using this strategy, be sure to still read all of the answer choices carefully and completely. If you feel unprepared, you should not attempt to predict the answers. This would be a waste of time and an opportunity for your mind to wander in the wrong direction.

2. Reading the Whole Question

Too often, test takers scan a multiple-choice question, recognize a few familiar words, and immediately jump to the answer choices. Test authors are aware of this common impatience, and they will sometimes prey upon it. For instance, a test author might subtly turn the question into a negative, or he or she might redirect the focus of the question right at the end. The only way to avoid falling into these traps is to read the entirety of the question carefully before reading the answer choices.

3. Looking for Wrong Answers

Long and complicated multiple-choice questions can be intimidating. One way to simplify a difficult multiple-choice question is to eliminate all of the answer choices that are clearly wrong. In most sets of answers, there will be at least one selection that can be dismissed right away. If the test is administered on paper, the test taker could draw a line through it to indicate that it may be ignored; otherwise, the test taker will have to perform this operation mentally or on scratch paper. In either case, once the obviously incorrect answers have been eliminated, the remaining choices may be considered. Sometimes identifying the clearly wrong answers will give the test taker some information about the correct answer. For instance, if one of the remaining answer choices is a direct opposite of one of the eliminated answer choices, it may well be the correct answer. The opposite of obviously wrong is obviously right! Of course, this is not always the case. Some answers are obviously incorrect simply because they are irrelevant to the question being asked. Still, identifying and eliminating some incorrect answer choices is a good way to simplify a multiple-choice question.

4. Don't Overanalyze

Anxious test takers often overanalyze questions. When you are nervous, your brain will often run wild, causing you to make associations and discover clues that don't actually exist. If you feel that this may be a problem for you, do whatever you can to slow down during the test. Try taking a deep breath or counting to ten. As you read and consider the question, restrict yourself to the particular words used by the author. Avoid thought tangents about what the author *really* meant, or what he or she was *trying* to say. The only things that matter on a multiple-choice test are the words that are actually in the question. You must avoid reading too much into a multiple-choice question, or supposing that the writer meant something other than what he or she wrote.

5. No Need for Panic

It is wise to learn as many strategies as possible before taking a multiple-choice test, but it is likely that you will come across a few questions for which you simply don't know the answer. In this situation, avoid panicking. Because most multiple-choice tests include dozens of questions, the relative value of a single wrong answer is small. As much as possible, you should compartmentalize each question on a multiple-choice test. In other words, you should not allow your feelings about one question to affect your success on the others. When you find a question that you either don't understand or don't know how to answer, just take a deep breath and do your best. Read the entire question slowly and carefully. Try rephrasing the question a couple of different ways. Then, read all of the answer choices carefully. After eliminating obviously wrong answers, make a selection and move on to the next question.

6. Confusing Answer Choices

When working on a difficult multiple-choice question, there may be a tendency to focus on the answer choices that are the easiest to understand. Many people, whether consciously or not, gravitate to the answer choices that require the least concentration, knowledge, and memory. This is a mistake. When you come across an answer choice that is confusing, you should give it extra attention. A question might be confusing because you do not know the subject matter to which it refers. If this is the case, don't eliminate the answer before you have affirmatively settled on another. When you come across an answer choice of this type, set it aside as you look at the remaining choices. If you can confidently assert that one of the other choices is correct, you can leave the confusing answer aside. Otherwise, you will need to take a moment to try to better understand the confusing answer choice. Rephrasing is one way to tease out the sense of a confusing answer choice.

7. Your First Instinct

Many people struggle with multiple-choice tests because they overthink the questions. If you have studied sufficiently for the test, you should be prepared to trust your first instinct once you have carefully and completely read the question and all of the answer choices. There is a great deal of research suggesting that the mind can come to the correct conclusion very quickly once it has obtained all of the relevant information. At times, it may seem to you as if your intuition is working faster even than your reasoning mind. This may in fact be true. The knowledge you obtain while studying may be retrieved from your subconscious before you have a chance to work out the associations that support it. Verify your instinct by working out the reasons that it should be trusted.

8. Key Words

Many test takers struggle with multiple-choice questions because they have poor reading comprehension skills. Quickly reading and understanding a multiple-choice question requires a mixture of skill and experience. To help with this, try jotting down a few key words and phrases on a piece of scrap paper. Doing this concentrates the process of reading and forces the mind to weigh the relative importance of the question's parts. In selecting words and phrases to write down, the test taker thinks about the question more deeply and carefully. This is especially true for multiple-choice questions that are preceded by a long prompt.

9. Subtle Negatives

One of the oldest tricks in the multiple-choice test writer's book is to subtly reverse the meaning of a question with a word like *not* or *except*. If you are not paying attention to each word in the question, you can easily be led astray by this trick. For instance, a common question format is, "Which of the following is...?" Obviously, if the question instead is, "Which of the following is not...?," then the answer will be quite different. Even worse, the test makers are aware of the potential for this mistake and will include one answer choice that would be correct if the question were not negated or reversed. A test taker who misses the reversal will find what he or she believes to be a correct answer and will be so confident that he or she will fail to reread the question and discover the original error. The only way to avoid this is to practice a wide variety of multiple-choice questions and to pay close attention to each and every word.

10. Reading Every Answer Choice

It may seem obvious, but you should always read every one of the answer choices! Too many test takers fall into the habit of scanning the question and assuming that they understand the question because they recognize a few key words. From there, they pick the first answer choice that answers the question they believe they have read. Test takers who read all of the answer choices might discover that one of the latter answer choices is actually *more* correct. Moreover, reading all of the answer choices can remind you of facts related to the question that can help you arrive at the correct answer. Sometimes, a misstatement or incorrect detail in one of the latter answer choices will trigger your memory of the subject and will enable you to find the right answer. Failing to read all of the answer choices is like not reading all of the items on a restaurant menu: you might miss out on the perfect choice.

11. Spot the Hedges

One of the keys to success on multiple-choice tests is paying close attention to every word. This is never truer than with words like almost, most, some, and sometimes. These words are called "hedges" because they indicate that a statement is not totally true or not true in every place and time. An absolute statement will contain no hedges, but in many subjects, the answers are not always straightforward or absolute. There are always exceptions to the rules in these subjects. For this reason, you should favor those multiple-choice questions that contain hedging language. The presence of qualifying words indicates that the author is taking special care with his or her words, which is certainly important when composing the right answer. After all, there are many ways to be wrong, but there is only one way to be right! For this reason, it is wise to avoid answers that are absolute when taking a multiple-choice test. An absolute answer is one that says things are either all one way or all another. They often include words like *every*, *always*, *best*, and *never*. If you are taking a multiple-choice test in a subject that doesn't lend itself to absolute answers, be on your guard if you see any of these words.

12. Long Answers

In many subject areas, the answers are not simple. As already mentioned, the right answer often requires hedges. Another common feature of the answers to a complex or subjective question are qualifying clauses, which are groups of words that subtly modify the meaning of the sentence. If the question or answer choice describes a rule to which there are exceptions or the subject matter is complicated, ambiguous, or confusing, the correct answer will require many words in order to be expressed clearly and accurately. In essence, you should not be deterred by answer choices that seem excessively long. Oftentimes, the author of the text will not be able to write the correct answer without offering some qualifications and modifications. Your job is to read the answer choices thoroughly and completely and to select the one that most accurately and precisely answers the question.

13. Restating to Understand

Sometimes, a question on a multiple-choice test is difficult not because of what it asks but because of how it is written. If this is the case, restate the question or answer choice in different words. This process serves a couple of important purposes. First, it forces you to concentrate on the core of the question. In order to rephrase the question accurately, you have to understand it well. Rephrasing the question will concentrate your mind on the key words and ideas. Second, it will present the information to your mind in a fresh way. This process may trigger your memory and render some useful scrap of information picked up while studying.

14. True Statements

Sometimes an answer choice will be true in itself, but it does not answer the question. This is one of the main reasons why it is essential to read the question carefully and completely before proceeding to the answer choices. Too often, test takers skip ahead to the answer choices and look for true statements. Having found one of these, they are content to select it without reference to the question above. Obviously, this provides an easy way for test makers to play tricks. The savvy test taker will always read the entire question before turning to the answer choices. Then, having settled on a correct answer choice, he or she will refer to the original question and ensure that the selected answer is relevant. The mistake of choosing a correct-but-irrelevant answer choice is especially common on questions related to specific pieces of objective knowledge. A prepared test taker will have a wealth of factual knowledge at his or her disposal, and should not be careless in its application.

15. No Patterns

One of the more dangerous ideas that circulates about multiple-choice tests is that the correct answers tend to fall into patterns. These erroneous ideas range from a belief that B and C are the most common right answers, to the idea that an unprepared test-taker should answer "A-B-A-C-A-D-A-B-A." It cannot be emphasized enough that pattern-seeking of this type is exactly the WRONG way to approach a multiple-choice test. To begin with, it is highly unlikely that the test maker will plot the correct answers according to some predetermined pattern. The questions are scrambled and delivered in a random order. Furthermore, even if the test maker was following a pattern in the assignation of correct answers, there is no reason why the test taker would know which pattern he or she was using. Any attempt to discern a pattern in the answer choices is a waste of time and a distraction from the real work of taking the test. A test taker would be much better served by extra preparation before the test than by reliance on a pattern in the answers.

FREE DVD OFFER

Don't forget that doing well on your exam includes both understanding the test content and understanding how to use what you know to do well on the test. We offer a completely FREE Test Taking Tips DVD that covers world class test taking tips that you can use to be even more successful when you are taking your test.

All that we ask is that you email us your feedback about your study guide. To get your **FREE Test Taking Tips DVD**, email freedvd@studyguideteam.com with "FREE DVD" in the subject line and the following information in the body of the email:

- The title of your study guide.
- Your product rating on a scale of 1-5, with 5 being the highest rating.
- Your feedback about the study guide. What did you think of it?
- Your full name and shipping address to send your free DVD.

Introduction to the aPHR Exam

Function of the Test

The Associate Professional in Human Resources (aPHR) is for professionals who are new to the HR career track and want to jumpstart their entrance into the HR profession. To be eligible to take the aPHR, one must have a high school diploma or the global equivalent to a high school diploma. The aPHR exam is a knowledge-based credential and is for those who wish to prove their knowledge of foundational Human Resources in a new career. As of January 31, 2018, 2,338 professionals hold the aPHR credential. There is an 85% pass rate for the aPHR.

Test Administration

Testing for the aPHR exam is offered year-round through computer-based testing at Pearson VUE testing centers. Before an exam appointment can be scheduled, test takers must complete a HRCI Application Process form at the Pearson VUE website. After the application is approved, 120 days are given to choose an exam date and location.

Those who wish to retest must wait 90 days, and they may take the exam no more than 3 times within a 365-day period. Testing accommodations are available to those who wish to make a request on the Pearson website.

Test Format

On testing day, candidates should arrive fifteen minutes early and bring a government-issued, non-expired, photo ID. All personal items will be placed in a locker, including mobile devices. There are no scheduled breaks while taking the HRCI exam, but test takers may take a break while the test is in process keeping in mind it will count against their allotted time.

The topics on the aPHR are HR Operations; Employee Relations; Recruitment and Selection; Compensation and Benefits; Human Resource Development and Retention; and Health, Safety, and Security. Below is a table with each topic and its percentage on the exam:

Topic	Percentage
HR Operations	38%
Employee Relations	16%
Recruitment and Selection	15%
Compensation and Benefits	14%
Human Resource Development and Retention	12%
Health, Safety, and Security	5%

The aPHR is 2 hours and 15 minutes long with 100 scored multiple-choice questions and 25 pretest questions.

Scoring

Score reports are displayed at the testing center after the exam, and official score reports will be sent to test takers a couple days after the exam through the online platform. A "digital badge" is given by the HRCI as the official certificate, which can be displayed on social media or websites. Scores are reported as pass or fail, and a scaled score of at least 500 is needed in order to pass the aPHR.

Recent Developments

The aPHR is HRCI's newest career certification, beginning in January 2016. HRCI also got rid of testing windows in April 2016, making it possible for candidates to take the exam at any time of the year.

HR Operations

Organizational Strategy

Quality leadership skills are essential to any organization, and thus leadership training is typically provided to mid and upper management professionals. Effective leadership skills include strategic thinking, solving problems as they come, and managing time in the most financially responsible manner. While these skills are essential, there are also more human characteristics that must be mentioned. A successful leader must have the ability to build confidence within his or her organization, obtain the trust of others, inspire others, and engender a sense of pride and purpose within his or her company.

Navigating the Organization

Work Roles

Competent human resources (HR) personnel are able to do the following:

- Develop job postings that clearly and concisely explain the responsibilities required by the job
- Have the educational qualifications and knowledge skillsets that will support managing those responsibilities
- Acquire the soft skills that will ensure potential candidates will be a good fit for the role.

Not only must hired candidates be able to carry out the requirements of the job, their personal interests factor into their productivity and happiness over the long-term. HR professionals may utilize a number of personality assessment tools to determine good fits between candidates and roles. Jobs within an organization are developed based on goals and objectives established by leadership to ensure that qualified employees perform duties that contribute to the overall interest of the organization. Finally, HR personnel work with those in leadership roles to influence a company culture that sets the tone for how employees behave during work hours and how they interact with subordinates, lateral colleagues, and superiors.

Successful Implementation of HR Initiatives

An organization's processes, systems, and policies will vary depending on the overall goals and function of an organization, but most HR initiatives focus on several key categories that intend to most effectively utilize the personnel within the organization. These include, but are not limited to, the following:

- Finding, hiring, and retaining qualified candidates
- Employee compensation and benefits (such as hourly pay, salary, health insurance, paid leave, disability benefits, pension, and other perks based on employee interests)
- Organizational and employee development activities (such as professional trainings)
- Termination and retirement tasks
- Risk management, such as drug screening employees and providing safety courses relevant to job functions

The details and successful implementation of these initiatives are largely subjective, beginning with understanding an organization's mission. This is often defined by an established mission statement or company vision. All HR initiatives should contribute to the advancement of the organization's mission.

Political Environment and Culture

How employees think and feel about a company is critical to an employer. If members of an organization have negative associations with it, it can be difficult to motivate them. The overall "mood" of an organization is known as its climate, and organizational climate cannot be directly controlled. However, climate is closely affected by work environment, company standards, interactions, and a general sense of "how things are done around here." All these factors add up to what is called organizational culture. So, if an employer wants to improve the company's climate, they need to make changes to the company culture.

Vision

For any organization to be successful, it must have a clear idea of what it's doing and where it's going. Mission and vision statements are two ways for an organization to verbalize its objectives. A mission statement focuses on the work of the organization on a day-to-day basis and answers the following questions:

- What do we do now?
- Why are we doing it?
- What makes us different from other companies?

A **vision statement** focuses on the organization's future goals and answers the following questions:

- What do we want to accomplish?
- Where do we aim to be in the future?

A successful **mission statement** should be clear and direct. In short, it states *why* the organization exists, and in turn guides its values, standards, and other organizing principles. For example, an organic restaurant might have the following mission statement: "To serve customers healthy meals made from the freshest, locally sourced organic ingredients." With this mission statement, the restaurant could decide to focus its efforts on building relationships with local farmers or staying up-to-date on health food trends.

A vision statement focuses on specific future goals, and in turn guides the steps that the organization will take to achieve them. The same restaurant might decide on the following vision statement: "To become a top-rated restaurant in the city." The restaurant can then design a plan accordingly, perhaps by focusing on marketing campaigns or inviting influential reviewers to dine at the restaurant.

Managing HR Initiatives

Project Requirements

Senior leadership plays a role in dictating project timelines and end goals for an organization, and HR initiatives can support the processes that bring forth outcomes through high-level project management. In the planning stage of projects, HR professionals will need to take into account the skills that are needed in order for projects to be completed. Additionally, they will need to consider factors like timeline development, establishing mini-goals and deliverables, the resources needed and associated costs (such as labor, time required, materials needed, and so on), risks that may need to be mitigated, and analyses that determine returns on investment (ROI) of resources. These are often intrapersonal activities that may require the input and cooperation of stakeholders from various departments across the organization. Therefore, to move project processes forward in the most productive manner, HR professionals should anticipate selecting the appropriate stakeholders and fostering positive communication between them.

Project Goals and Progress Milestones

Project goals are stepping stones toward organizational goals, and projects are comprised of milestones that indicate outcome success. Milestones are progressive in nature and influence the general timeline of the project. In order to be useful, both goals and milestones should exhibit SMART qualities. SMART is a commonly used acronym in goal and milestone setting that states an effective end point should be Specific, Measurable, Achievable, Relevant, and Timely. This ensures the goal or milestone is detailed, can produce data to show evidence of its effectiveness, can feasibly be attained, is relevant to the organizational goal at hand, and occurs at appropriate and useful intervals that benefit the project. When developing project goals, HR personnel should be able to address each of the five SMART aspects. Often, these values are documented before the project begins.

Project Budgets and Resources

A project can require a wide array of resources depending on its scope. Beyond the number of personnel needed and their individual compensation packages, resource costs also include time spent, materials, potential trainings needed, long-term sustaining actions, and so on. Costs can be categorized into direct costs, which impact one project specifically (such as labor and materials), and indirect costs, which may affect specific projects but also serve the organization as a whole (such as leadership salary and permanent office furniture). These costs can be fixed, or they can vary over time. Developing a budget includes reviewing a project proposal fully and anticipating all projected costs over the completion of the project. These may be divided into chronological milestones (such as monthly, quarterly, or annually) or by outcome benchmarks (such as when a department is fully staffed or when a component of a product is developed). Budgets and resources should remain flexible and be updated as needed.

Overcoming Project Obstacles

No project is likely to be without obstacles. Anticipating potential obstacles and preparing for them can help the project remain on track for completion. Start-up plans should be reviewed and revised throughout the course of the project to account for any unexpected changes. Most importantly, these revisions must be communicated to project members. Most often, obstacles arise when team members do not have the skillset or resources to contribute to their role, when the content and timeline of deliverables are not clear or documented, and when communication from relevant leadership and between colleagues is lacking. Beginning the project with SMART attributes and allowing for communication with project staff and key stakeholders can reduce any obstacles that should arise. While some obstacles may be out of the organization's control (such as a sudden loss of external funding), internal obstacles can often be mitigated with appropriate contingency planning.

Necessary Resources

Once a project outcome has been identified, finding the resources needed to see the project to fruition is key. Allocating resources is a balancing act. Utilizing too many resources will lead to waste, but utilizing too few resources can result in delays, errors, or other obstacles. Skilled HR personnel will know how to produce the best value from the least resources—a concept based on the Lean approach, which was once used primarily in manufacturing. HR personnel can examine internal data from similar projects to anticipate what resources other initiatives might need. Tools from the Six Sigma approach, such as process mapping and value stream mapping, can also help objectively determine the resources needed at each step of the project and the actual value-add associated with them.

Resource Allocation

Milestones can serve as an indicator of when resources are inconsistent with project needs. If deliverables are not fulfilled by an established milestone, HR personnel may choose to examine the role of the resources that are in use. A gap analysis, a root cause analysis, or a cause-and-effect diagram, which pinpoint why an expected outcome was not met, can review discrepancies between expected and actual performances. Often, these indicate that there is a constraint in one or more resources, such as lack of material, lack of qualified employees, or lack of time. Once the resource in question has been addressed, implementing a test of change may show if shifting resources allows established milestones to be met. If not, this may indicate that components of the timeline for the project are not reasonable. Milestones, outcomes, or the construction of the timeline itself may require revision.

Project Adaptability

Project requirements, goals, and constraints are developed and anticipated during the planning stage. They are, however, subject to changes that may or may not be in the team's control. Changes in funding, personnel, and regulation, are examples of items that often cannot be fully accounted for during the project planning stage. HR project managers may benefit from managing their own expectations during the project planning stage, and by accepting that all baseline plans are fluid. Project plans should be continuously reviewed, and they should be revised when unexpected changes arise. Developing contingency processes during the project planning stage, cross-training team members, and developing the ability to critically and creatively think about new solutions are ways to mitigate unanticipated changes. Becoming aware of the professional strengths and weaknesses of team members and drawing on this knowledge during times of change can also help to fill gaps. These techniques allow the entire team to cohesively demonstrate agility and adaptability when needed.

Influence

HR Expert

There are numerous ways to build credibility as an HR expert, like having a formal educational background in industrial organization and related fields, such as psychology, project management, business, and communication. Continuing education after formal schooling, such as through earning certifications through nationally recognized credentialing bodies, is another way to further develop one's theoretical skillset. Staying abreast of literature pertaining to topics relevant to human resources is yet another avenue to illustrate professional expertise. From a practical standpoint, using one's knowledge to offer solutions to personnel issues within the organization is a way to showcase credibility. Sharing success stories with colleagues in the field can build professional credibility outside of one's organization.

Promoting Buy-In

The most effective way to promote buy-in among organizational stakeholders for HR initiatives is to show the added value of an initiative to the stakeholders, employees, and organization as a whole. Added value will need to be large enough that it is worth the associated costs of implementing the initiative. To this end, HR personnel who are proposing initiatives have the responsibility of understanding what outcomes each of their stakeholders perceives as valuable. An initiative that the HR team finds valuable may not have meaning for stakeholders. Often, stakeholders consist of leadership personnel whose buy-in is necessary for the initiative to be approved. Leadership buy-in is also crucial in order to successfully implement change (known as top-down change), otherwise gaining subordinate approval proves extremely challenging. Finally, determining what is of value may vary across departments. Therefore, finding umbrella goals or interest overlaps can be useful.

Motivating HR Staff

An effective leader understands that team motivation is influenced by a number of factors, and that some fall outside the leader's locus of influence. The first step in motivating HR staff is ensuring that candidates who are passionate about the field, the organization, and the organization's interests are hired as staff. Candidates who are not a good professional or cultural fit for the team may be difficult to motivate, may be unhappy on the job, and may not find success within the organization. Ensuring that qualified employees remain motivated may include providing opportunities for professional growth, recognizing and rewarding professional excellence, promoting work-life satisfaction, and creating an open, encouraging, and positive work environment. Motivating other stakeholders to support HR's visions and goals is most likely to include continuous highlights of the value that the department provides to both the stakeholder as an individual, and to the organization as a whole. This may be expressed in program evaluations, reports, presentations, graphs, anecdotal evidence, or employee testimonials.

Advocacy

HR personnel are responsible for managing the productivity and welfare of an organization's employees, but also for ensuring that employees are able to safely perform their jobs in a way that advances the organization's interests. It can be a balancing act to manage employee needs with business needs, especially during times when one side needs more than the other (such as if an essential employee has to take an extended medical leave, or if a valued business customer needs a complex product on short notice). It is also important that employees do not take advantage of the organization, and vice versa. HR personnel are often in charge of developing guidelines that help to regulate these dual needs; these are often documented in a company handbook that is accessible to all employees. Guidelines may be established for instances such as leaves of absence, overtime, meal breaks, harassment, and other contexts specific to the industry.

Establishing Relationships: Outside Organizations

As much as organizations must understand and analyze their internal operations, they must also look outward and engage with the industry as a whole. This is equally true of HR relationships, which should be fostered both within and outside of the organization. By building external relationships, HR professionals can stay abreast of industry developments, develop innovative solutions, and be active (or even proactive) members of their field.

Corporate Social Responsibility (CSR)

Corporate Social Responsibility (CSR) refers to an organization's sense of responsibility for its impact on the environment and community. CSR can be evaluated based on the three Ps of the "triple bottom line": people, planet, and profit. *People* refers to fair employment practices as well as the organization's impact on members of the community; *planet* refers to the organization's environmental impact (such as pollution, consumption of natural resources, etc.); and *profit* refers to the organization's overall contribution to economic growth. Having a CSR program encourages an organization to operate within legal, moral, and ethical boundaries. From an HR perspective, an organization's CSR program can also affect employee recruiting because the program demonstrates the organization's commitment to fair working conditions.

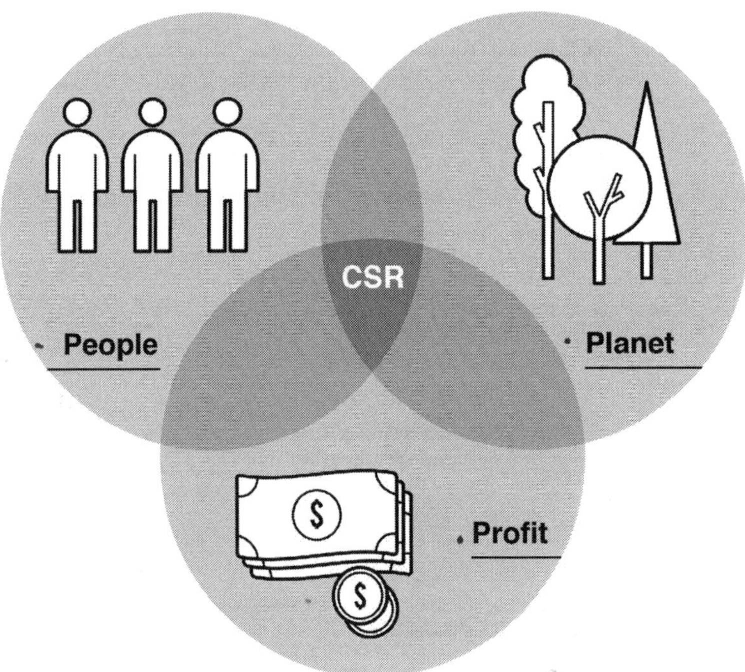

Community Partnership

In addition to financial capital, organizations also rely on **social capital**, the community's relationship with, and attitude toward, the organization. An organization can boost its social capital by engaging community partners from schools to social or volunteer groups to other organizations. These partnerships demonstrate an organization's commitment to the community in which it operates and offer an opportunity for community members to develop a closer relationship with the organization. For example, a computer networking company might partner with the local public school system to offer a free summer camp program for high school students interested in computers.

Organizational Culture

A team-oriented organizational culture is one that actively views professional efforts as a group accomplishment. Individualistic terms (such as "I achieved this" versus "We achieved this") are rarely used. Knowing each team member's strengths and leveraging those when establishing project responsibilities promotes effective use of resources. However, implementing cross-training sessions to address weaknesses also helps to establish a strong team unit by allowing members to feel as though they can support one another in times of need. All members should feel accountable for their work in the team. This can be achieved through documenting expectations for each member and discussing how individual objectives integrate to create results. Finally, resources that support team culture (such as physical space in the organization to accommodate groups) should be available.

How employees think and feel about a company is critical to an employer. If members of an organization have negative associations with it, it can be difficult to motivate them. The overall "mood" of an organization is known as its climate, and organizational climate cannot be directly controlled. However, climate is closely affected by work environment, company standards, interactions, and a general sense of "how things are done around here." All these factors add up to what is called organizational culture. So, if an employer wants to improve the company's climate, they need to make changes to the company culture.

Encouraging Communication and Involvement

Encouraging communication and involvement is often a step in the right direction toward changing company culture. And much like climate and culture, communication and involvement are closely related, but not necessarily identical. For example, if John's boss gives him increased responsibility over an aspect of his work, then John has become more involved. However, if John still has no input from his boss on the decision process or has no formal way to share his ideas with management, then the boss has not encouraged communication. Conversely, if John's boss starts sending regular memos detailing company activities and the strategies behind them, this is an increase in communication. However, if John and other employees have no way to act or contribute to this knowledge, then the boss has not encouraged involvement. To make meaningful changes to company culture, both communication and involvement should be addressed.

Involvement Strategies

There are numerous involvement strategies that companies can use. For example, the act of delegating authority allows an employee to make more decisions. By granting people more responsibility, an employer can encourage them to take a greater sense of ownership over a company's successes. An **employee survey** can be used to ask employees how they feel about the company. Surveys can be formal (written or online) or informal (simply asking around), and can address topics such as concerns, suggestions for improvement, and priorities. It should be noted that, even in an anonymous survey, employees may feel hesitant to share their true feelings if the workplace culture is viewed as unfriendly.

In addition to surveys, a **suggestion program**, via an idea box or an online submission form, allows employees to recommend ways to address company problems. Unlike a survey, a suggestion program is an ongoing part of company involvement. Employees can also work together in a formal capacity as part of a committee to address company concerns. Committees may be temporary or ongoing, and employees' service on a committee may also be for a specific term or a permanent appointment.

Moreover, an **employee-management committee** is a specific kind of committee where employees work alongside management to address company concerns. Sometimes known as employee participation groups, these committees also can be temporary or ongoing, depending on the needs of the organization. Finally, employees can also serve on a task force, which is similar to a committee but focused on a specific problem and is usually temporary in nature. Employees on a task force work to determine the cause of a problem and work to develop a solution.

Legal and Regulatory Environment

HR professionals need to be familiar with relevant employment laws and regulations. Applicable laws may vary based on organization type, size, and other factors, but there are many regulations that apply to the majority of organizations. Several important regulations are administered by the Equal Employment Opportunity Commission, or EEOC. One of these is Title VII of the Civil Rights Act of 1964, which applies to employers with fifteen or more employees and prohibits discrimination based on race, color, religion, sex, or national origin. EEOC also oversees the Age Discrimination in Employment Act of 1967 (ADEA), which prohibits discrimination against anyone forty years old or older in terms of hiring, promotion, wages, termination, and denial of benefits. The ADEA also prohibits mandatory retirement in many sectors. The Equal Pay Act (EPA) prohibits wage discrimination based on sex for people in the same organization performing the same or similar jobs (in terms of skills and responsibilities) under the same or similar conditions. In addition, the EEOC administers ADA, discussed earlier in this study guide.

Domestic and Global Employment Laws

Other important regulations include the Fair Labor Standard Act (FLSA) which establishes things like minimum wage and overtime pay, standards for child labor, and defining exempt and non-exempt employees. The Family and Medical Leave Act (FMLA) outlines standards for when employees are permitted to take unpaid, job-protected family and medical leave. The Occupational Safety and Health Act of 1970 created the Occupational Safety and Health Administration (OSHA), which ensures that employers provide a safe and healthy workplace. This includes things like eliminating or reducing hazards when possible, providing free safety equipment, informing employees about chemical hazards, providing comprehensive and comprehensible safety training, keeping records of work-related injuries and illnesses, and displaying the official OSHA poster describing employees' rights and employers' responsibilities.

Alignment of HR Programs, Practices, and Policies

HR programs, practices, and policies must align and comply with these laws and regulations and others. This means staying current on local, state, and federal regulations, as well as any international laws that may be applicable. It also means being proactive and circumspect about where laws need to be applied. This ensures that the organization is providing a safe and fair workplace for employees, while also ensuring that the organization avoids any fees, fines, lawsuits, or other liabilities that may arise from not following the law. For example, when posting a job advertisement, HR must ensure that there are no references to restricting hiring based on things like age, race, or sex. The same applies to the interviewing and hiring stages, even until terminating employees.

Illegal and Noncompliant HR-Related Behaviors

Because these decisions and practices can extend beyond HR, HR professionals are also responsible for coaching employees at all levels about how to avoid illegal and noncompliant behaviors. One way to keep employees informed is by displaying posters related to applicable laws and regulations; as previously mentioned, employers are required to display certain information (related to things like OSHA and FLSA), depending on such factors as the size, location, and type of organization. The U.S. Department of Labor (DOL) offers resources to help organizations determine what information they are legally obligated to display for employees. HR can also coach employees who are responsible for things like hiring and terminating decisions in order to avoid illegal terminations, for example, or illegal questions during job interviews. Interviewers should be sure to ask only questions that are job-related and determine qualifications that are justified by a business purpose (also known as bona fide occupational qualification, or BFOQ). If interviewers and hiring managers are screening employees based on factors that are not covered by BFOQ, it can present grounds for complaints of discrimination (for example, when an employer requires a higher level of education than is necessary for a position, and then uses this requirement as a basis to screen applicants of certain racial or socioeconomic backgrounds).

Interpretation of Employment Laws

HR professionals can also consult legal experts as needed when it comes to the interpretation and application of employment laws. Whether those legal services are internal or external may depend on the nature of the organization. Smaller organizations may be more likely to consult with outside services, while large organizations are more like to have in-house legal services. However, particularly when an organization begins operation in a new area (for example, in a new state or country), it would be a prudent move to consult with experts who have experience in local laws.

Confidentiality and Privacy Rules

Secure data storage is a difficult but necessary policy to prevent corruption from malware and hackers. Data corruption is a widespread concern for firms of all sizes and locations. Organizations with sensitive and confidential data, such as government agencies, continue to take steps to strengthen their data security. Data backup requires copying and archiving current information to separate drives to restore information in the event of data corruption. Data storage and backup are essential to protect organizational plans, policies, and secrets in the event of a data breach.

Business Functions

In order to understand its performance, evaluate which strategies are effective, and identify where improvement is needed, an organization must regularly analyze internal business information. Data is analyzed using **metrics** (sometimes known as key performance indicators). A metric is simply a method of measuring a particular set of data. Different metrics can be applied to different areas of an organization.

For accounting and finance, metrics are essential for evaluating an organization's financial status.

Cash flow metrics are concerned with analyzing money coming in and going out. One straightforward cash flow metric is net cash flow, which measures the difference between incoming and outgoing cash over a fixed period (e.g. monthly, annually). Net cash flow can provide an immediate answer to the question, "Are we gaining or losing money over this period of time?" By reviewing this metric, an organization can determine if any strategic planning changes are necessary, particularly if the organization is losing more money than expected.

Another cash flow metric is **return on investment**, or **ROI**. ROI is generally expressed as a ratio or percentage comparing the gains of a particular investment with its initial investment price. In other words, ROI measures the ratio between an investment's profit and its cost. ROI is particularly useful in helping an organization evaluate the overall value of a given investment. For example, one investment may yield a high return, but perhaps the initial investment is costly as well. Another investment with a much lower yield also has a far lower initial cost—so the cheaper investment might actually have a higher ROI than the high-return investment. This metric can help an organization to devote its financial resources to investments with the highest ROI.

Shareholders might be especially concerned with an organization's **return on equity**, or **ROE**. Like ROI, ROE is also expressed as a ratio or percentage. This ratio can be found by dividing a company's fiscal year net income by the total shareholder equity. The purpose of this metric is to demonstrate how efficiently a company uses investments to generate profit by measuring the company's rate of return on its shareholders' equity. It can give shareholders confidence that their investment is being well-used—or it can tell them to invest their money elsewhere. In order to evaluate its competitiveness, a company can compare its ROE with that of other companies in its field. If the comparison is unfavorable, then it's time to make some strategic planning adjustments.

For marketing and sales, metrics can indicate if a particular marketing strategy is succeeding or if it must be reevaluated. As with financial metrics, there's a wide range of marketing and sales metrics. Let's focus on a few of the most useful categories.

First, many sales and marketing metrics focus on leads. A **lead** is any person or group who interacts with the organization and might become a customer or client. For example, an online shopping mall might consider anyone who registers an account or joins their mailing list to be a lead. Some helpful metrics consider lead volume (the total number of leads at any given time) or leads generated (the total number of new leads gained during a fixed period, useful for evaluating whether a new marketing strategy is drawing more leads). Sales are like a funnel: the lead volume is wide at the top and then slowly narrows as the sales team nurtures leads into profitable customers. So another leads-related metric includes lead-to-customer percentage (also known as a lead conversion), or the ratio of lead volume to new customers. This allows an organization to gauge the effectiveness of its sales team.

Another important metric is **average transaction value** *(***ATV***)*. This metric measures the average amount that one customer spends on one transaction. To return to the example of the online shopping mall, perhaps their ATV is $45—on average, each customer spends $45 when they place an order. This metric allows the online shop to predict its revenue by multiplying the ATV by the anticipated number of customers during a set period. Analyzing this metric also presents different marketing options to increase revenue—the organization can choose to focus on drawing more customers or on increasing the ATV of current customers. Some strategies to increase ATV are to offer rewards programs or special sales to established customers.

Finally, many helpful metrics relate to sales cost. How much money is spent on sales? Is a sales strategy cost-effective? The gross profit margin for a period can be found by subtracting the cost of sales from the total revenue and then dividing that number by the total revenue. This metric shows if a current sales strategy is actually effective and profitable. Another metric is the customer acquisition cost, or the amount spent getting a new customer. Analyzing the ratio between a customer's lifetime value (LTV) and the customer acquisition cost (CAC) can reveal whether current sales strategies are too costly compared to the overall value of a particular customer.

Operations and Business Development

There are also many important metrics related to operations and business development. Three important ones highlighted here are the number of activities, the opportunity success rate, and the innovation rate.

When measuring the **number of activities**, an activity is any task currently undertaken by the organization. This metric can show whether an organization is properly investing its resources in profitable work or if it's overextending its resources into too many tasks. Multi-tasking and diversifying are important in developing a business, but taking on too many activities can hinder an organization's performance.

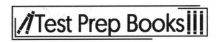

The **opportunity success rate** overlaps somewhat with the sales and marketing metrics described above. In this sense, an opportunity is a halfway point between a lead and a customer—the lead has been contacted by the sales team but isn't yet a customer. The opportunity success rate measures how many opportunities are closed by sales. This metric can help marketing and sales strategies as well as the overall business development plan. If the opportunity success rate is high, the organization can easily bring in new customers and develop its business. If the opportunity success rate is low, the organization might focus on developing current customers rather than spending resources on new ones.

A third metric to keep in mind is the **innovation rate**. Innovation includes any new or improved products and services. To find the innovation rate, divide the revenue generated by new products and services by the total revenue from all products and services over a given period. This allows the organization to see how much of an impact innovation has on its overall operations, and whether more resources must be devoted to developing innovative ideas that will give the organization an edge over its competition.

Information Technology

Nowadays, organizations rely on information technology to carry out essential business functions. Some conduct the entirety of their business via the internet. These metrics can help organizations get the most out of their IT departments.

One important category analyzes the functionality of an organization's IT resources. That is, how well are IT services working? This can be measured by looking at the number of software bugs over a given period, or the average number of hours required to resolve IT issues. If there's a large volume of IT problems, or if it takes too long to fix critical IT issues, the organization must devote more resources to improving its IT functionality.

IT metrics can also consider online business activities that examine an organization's online sales presence. If a business has a website, one important metric is the number of page views. This measures the organization's reach—how many potential customers is the organization reaching through its online marketing? How many page views lead to actual purchases? How many visitors are registered on the site or subscribed to a newsletter? If the organization isn't satisfied with this number, it's time to try new online marketing strategies. The business can also look at the ratio of online sales to sales from non-internet business (for example, over the phone or in person) in order to determine where it should focus sales and marketing efforts.

Finally, as with any department, organizations must consider the cost of IT. This metric helps the organization see what portion of its financial resources is devoted to IT services, and whether this investment adds value to the organization. For example, an organization may invest in new project management software, but this software increases productivity and helps managers keep project costs low—so the cost of the software is offset by the savings it creates.

HR Policies and Procedures

Americans with Disabilities Act

The Americans with Disabilities Act (ADA) is a federal law that outlaws discrimination based on disability. The ADA precludes discrimination based on race, sex, national origin, and religion. Moreover, the law requires that employers provide reasonable accommodations to employees who have a disability. For instance, this could require employers to build a wheelchair accessible ramp for disabled employers to enter and leave the building. Also, the ADA stipulates that public spaces be accessible for disabled persons. Under this law, all employees are guaranteed equal access to career development and training.

Additionally, all employees are also guaranteed equal access to career development and training under the Age Discrimination in Employment Act (ADEA) and the Uniformed Services Employment and Reemployment Rights Act (USERRA).

Equal Opportunity Employment (EEO) Reporting

Annual workforce data reporting is required by the Equal Employment Opportunity Commission (EEOC) for all employers with one hundred or more employees and federal contractors with at least fifty employees and contracts of $50,000. The reports are due each year by September 30. In addition, these employers must place EEO posters and notices in prominent locations within their workplaces. EEO reporting aids employers in determining their workforce composition, to ensure they are not discriminating against protected classes.

The various EEO reports collect data by some type of job grouping about race/ethnicity and gender. There are nine EEO job reporting categories:

- Officials and managers
- Professionals
- Technicians
- Sales
- Office and clerical
- Craft workers (skilled)
- Operatives (semiskilled)
- Laborers (unskilled)
- Service workers

As an example, the EEO-1 Report, which is also known as the Employer Information Report, categorizes data by race/ethnicity, gender, and job category. This report applies to employers who are required to file an annual report of employee sex and race/ethnic categories under Title VII of the 1964 Civil Rights Act. Government guidelines for the reporting of race are detailed in the EEO1 report form, which is jointly produced by the EEOC and the Office of Federal Contract Compliance.

Progressive Discipline

Progressive discipline is a system that, rather than defining a single "one size fits all" response to an employee infraction, attempts to address each incident as a unique situation, and then develops consequences accordingly. Typically, factors like severity and frequency (in other words, "how bad" and "how often") are key in determining the appropriate response. Many organizations make use of a five-stage process. Coaching is the first stage, where the manager discusses the behavior problem with the employee. This stage is typically used for small or first-time infractions. Then the employee receives a first warning. This is also called the counseling stage and usually involves the employee receiving a verbal warning. Then the second warning follows, which is also called the formal warning stage. This stage progresses to the employee receiving a written warning. A disciplinary action follows. At this stage, the employee is suspended for his or her behavior. Finally, if the chain of progressive discipline has not corrected the behavior, the final step in the progressive discipline process is to terminate the individual's employment.

HR Metrics

Cost per Hire

The cost per hire is calculated by adding together the external and internal recruiting costs and dividing that amount by the total number of new hires during a specific time period. Examples of external recruiting costs include items such as: advertising the position on job boards, recruitment outsourcing, recruitment technology, background checks and drug testing, and pre-hire assessments. Examples of internal recruiting costs include such items as: in-house recruiting staff, payment of referral rewards, and internal recruiting systems.

Selection Ratios

There are a number of different selection ratios used to evaluate recruitment sources. For example, to find the percentage of qualified applicants, the number of qualified applicants is divided by the number of total applicants for a particular position. The percentage of minority applicants is calculated by taking the number of minority applicants divided by the total number of applicants for a position. Additionally, the percentage of offers accepted is the number of offers accepted divided by the number of offers that were extended.

Adverse Impact

There are two types of discrimination: disparate treatment and disparate or adverse impact. Disparate treatment occurs when an employer treats protected classes differently than other employees. Examples of disparate treatment include holding genders to different standards, sexual harassment, and blatantly rejecting a member of a protected class due to stereotypes.

A famous disparate treatment case was McDonnell Douglas Corporation vs. Green. Green was a black employee who was laid off during a regular reduction in force. He protested at the company (as part of a group), chained and locked company doors, and blocked an entrance to company property. His activities did not please the company. When the company began hiring again, they advertised, and Green reapplied. He was denied, and the company continued looking for candidates. Green claimed the rejection was due to his race and his involvement in civil rights activities. This was a precedent-setting EEO case that established criteria for disparate treatment and ruled that a *prima facie* (at first glance) case can be shown if an employee:

- Belongs to a protected class
- Applied for a job when the employer sought applicants
- Was qualified and yet rejected
- Was rejected but the employer kept looking

In disparate treatment cases, an individual must prove:

- They are a member of a protected class
- They applied for a job for which they were qualified and for which the employer was seeking applicants
- They were not hired even though they were qualified
- After they did not get the job, the position remained open and the employer continued to receive applications

Disparate or **adverse impact** refers to a form of discrimination where an employer's policy seems neutral but in fact has an adverse impact on a certain group or a certain characteristic such as race, sex, or disability. This was identified by the Supreme Court in 1971 in the case of Griggs v. Duke Power Co., where it was proven that the requirement of a high school diploma for higher-paid positions was unfairly affecting African-American employees in lower-paid labor positions who had a history of receiving inferior education.

As another example, if an employer requires a potential employee for a position to be at least 5'10", it may exclude an entire group, such as women. Because statistically men are taller, this requirement is based solely on biological reasons rather than if the candidate can adequately perform the required role.

An employer discriminating based on certain physical elements, however, can be justified if it is in correlation with job requirements. For example, it is necessary for a fire department to discriminate based on height, facial hair, or grooming to ensure the safety of its employees.

Turnover Statistics

Turnover is typically calculated on either a monthly or an annual basis. Analyzing turnover is necessary to accurately forecast the number of new employees that are needed to replace individuals who have recently moved out of job positions. To calculate turnover, the number of separations per year is divided by the average number of individuals employed per month, multiplied by 100. For example, if fifty individuals separated during the year and there is an average of two hundred individuals employed per month, the turnover rate is:

$$\frac{50}{200} \times 100 = 25\%$$

Number of Grievances

Human resources (HR) often tracks the number and percentage of grievances received per employee. These numbers enable HR to establish a grievance rate and determine whether there are larger issues that need to be addressed. Grievance costs are also an important metric to monitor. For example, if a grievance is continually being filed because the incorrect individual is being selected to work overtime shifts, this could result in having to pay the employee(s) who should have been offered this opportunity. This could be a huge cost that the organization must absorb with nothing to show for it. In these cases, it is important to address the reason for the grievances and resolve the underlying issue. A simple misunderstanding or inaccurate interpretation of the process may be causing the issue. Tracking the grievances based on subject matter is also important to address the root causes of problems and implement solutions that will make an impact and correct the concerns. Additionally, grievances should be tracked to show what the closing time is—when the grievance is filed and when the grievance is closed. Average close times vary, depending on the issue, and HR may want to implement target close times to improve performance. Tracking grievances can also indicate the health of the relationship between management and the labor union. Decreased grievances across the board can show there is a focus on employee relations.

Tools to Compile Data

Organizations often implement systems or software specific to HR functions. These tools can allow easier access to and downloading of data. HR can then use the downloaded data to review it for various purposes. Excel spreadsheets can be a vital tool for HR. From analyzing average or median compensation data for salary surveys, to determining which employees are eligible to retire for succession planning purposes, to running a mail merge with Microsoft Word of mailing addresses to send out a newsletter, spreadsheets can be an extremely useful and effective tool. Human resources management systems (HRMS) provide many services to an organization in one platform; they can handle employee information such as personal data, payroll functions such as issues with paychecks, training schedules and rosters to ensure compliance with mandated training, and compensation data to evaluate an employee's salary. HRMS platforms often have a custom report program as well. These platforms usually allow users to download the data from the system to an Excel spreadsheet for further analysis and review. Reports can be run that show many different topics and status, including:

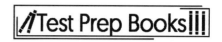

- Types of employees (full-time, part-time, limited-term)
- Employee demographics (male/female, over/under 40, years of service, retirement eligible)
- Compensation Information (last increase, annual wage)
- Training Records (mandated training, voluntary training)
- Open positions (recruitment needs)

This information can be vital when:

- Preparing budget and headcount reports and analysis
- Preparing company overview information for prospective applicants
- Initiating voluntary retirement programs
- Preparing succession plans
- Planning service awards and recognizing milestone anniversaries
- Analyzing compensation for salary surveys and reviews
- Ensuring compliance with mandated training as well as required training for certain positions
- Determining recruitment strategies

By having accurate information available quickly, HR can properly assess multiple areas to ensure effective strategies are implemented to address them.

Methods to Collect Data

Data Advocate

Using Data to Inform Business Decisions

Data that is collected from reliable, relevant, and unbiased sources can provide a tremendous amount of objective information from which evidence-based, logical decisions can be made. Therefore, good data can provide a number of benefits to business and non-profit organizations. Data can provide information about consumer trends, customer preferences, client engagement, and advertising techniques. Internally, data can provide information about employees, including productivity trends and influencers, job satisfaction, the effects of specific performance rewards and benefits, turnover rates, and so forth. This information can then be further explored to develop and implement process changes that affect how business operations take place; how employees are recruited, trained, and rewarded; and how the organization impacts its surrounding environment. A number of data collection, management, and analytical tools that convert raw data into clear trends are available for use. This allows even individuals who have limited background experience using statistical methods to learn how to best leverage information available within the organization.

Evidence-Based Decision Making

Evidence-based decision-making is a concept that utilizes information grounded in statistically significant data, peer-reviewed scholarly research, the reported values and preferences of stakeholders, and reputable anecdotes of industry experts to drive industrial, organizational, or scientific efforts. When HR professionals make decisions based on evidence, they provide credibility and logical support to their endeavors as they can show that such decisions have had consistent prior success. Published evidence also provides transparency—a vital component of communication that builds trust—as to why certain decisions are made; it can be easily communicated to and shared with employees who are interested. Utilizing established, proven information to drive decisions is also associated with outcomes that are of higher quality and less prone to failures or errors. Finally, evidence-based decision-making allows the process to be a collaboration between leadership personnel, individuals who are affected by the decision, and other stakeholders as necessary. This can be an empowering practice for all parties involved.

Validating HR Programs, Practices, and Policies

Validation as it relates to HR programs, practices, and policies refers to monitoring their step-by-step processes from start to finish to ensure that the same, desired output occurs every time. They should be regularly audited for strict operating parameters, controlled processes, and clearly-defined outcomes within each of these categories. Validation ensures that a program, practice, or policy delivers results in a consistent and predictable manner. Each of these aspects of HR should be reviewed at periodic intervals to ensure that they are still valid, as variable circumstances such as employee changes, regulatory reforms, customer preferences, and environmental factors are inputs which can influence process validity. When process validation is compromised and products or services are not produced in a consistent manner with expected specifications, there is an increased risk to product or service quality. In turn, this can translate to poor customer or stakeholder experiences, failure to meet expected deliverables or metrics, and an overall waste of resources.

Decision Points Informed by Data and Evidence

Decision points for which large sets of clean, relevant data exist should always draw upon analytics of the data to drive decision-making. Analytics software can analyze large data sets for trends that show how certain decisions have played out historically. Additionally, external studies conducted by universities or other research groups may have published manuscripts that provide relevant evidence to guide a decision. When HR professionals finds themselves at a point where an organizational decision needs to be made, they should first examine if any data or published research exists that could indicate best practices relevant for the decision at hand. If absolutely no data or published research on the topic exists, HR professionals have a responsibility to make an educated hypothesis to drive decision-making, implement a test of change, and gather relevant data along the course of the initiative that can be later analyzed. Outcomes should be shared with colleagues.

Data Gathering

Data Collection, Research Methods, Benchmarks, and HR Metrics

Data collection should procure information that is relevant to the process or outcome of interest. Quality assurance is the process of establishing a relevant, unbiased system of data collection. HR professionals must define data to be collected (i.e., qualitative, quantitative, anecdotal), standardize collection processes and instruments, and train data collectors. Data collection should be free from bias, confounders, unethical practices, and any other influences that skew the reliability and validity of the data. When possible, data collection should be random, objective, and standardized to the greatest extent. HR professionals will need to understand basics of different research design methods (i.e., experimental, observational) in order to select the most appropriate one for the context. Benchmarks and HR metrics should guide the type of research design and data collection utilized. For example, a metric focused on employee satisfaction will collect data differently than a metric focused on employee absenteeism.

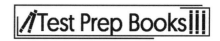

Solving Organizational Problems and Answering Questions

When using data to solve organizational problems and answer questions, HR professionals can expect to come across less than ideal sources. These sources of data may be factually inaccurate, collected with poor research design methods, irrelevant to the interest at hand, biased, or otherwise ineffectual. HR professionals should turn to high quality, reputable sources of data and data synthesis before reviewing it and relevant studies. This can include internal sources, such as a data information or statistics team within the organization whose sole purpose it is to collect and analyze data, or external sources, such as academic journals or industry renowned publications. HR professionals should ensure that data and studies are recent (ideally collected or published within the past three years). Meaningful data should be statistically significant, answer questions of interest, and come from a controlled collection mechanism. All sources should be cited and dated to provide complete context.

Data Gathering

Data collection methods will vary based on the type of solution or review process that is needed. Surveys can be used to gather individual feedback from a wide demographic. They can be conducted in person, online, or over the telephone; however, they are subject to interviewer bias, voluntary completion, and low completion rates. Focus groups utilize the services of a skilled facilitator who solicits feedback and opinions about a specific topic from identified stakeholders. Focus groups run the risk of low engagement or facilitator bias. Observational data collection utilizes one data collector to observe a specific context and take notes; however, this is highly subject to bias if the data collector is visible. Other types of data collection can be quantitative, such as records of sales, customer satisfaction scores, number of process failures, or returning clients. If an organization maintains diligent data management practices, these can usually serve as easily accessible sources of information. Permission to use personal information is normally required.

Relevant Data in External Sources

External sources for data relevant to the organization can include reputable news sources, highly regarded digital and paper publications, key note speakers and workshops at industry-specific conferences, discussions at high-level networking events, and data disseminated by successful competitors or colleagues. HR professionals should note any threats or opportunities that may present from competing organizations, demographic changes in the organization's geographic region, new relevant federal or state regulations, consumer trends relevant to their organization's products or services, changes in technology or innovation that could impact the organization's operations and output, potential environmental factors that could affect the organization's productivity, shifts in political climate and social culture, and so on. This type of information can be organized into a PESTLE chart or SWOT analysis to best review the potential impact to the organization. HR professionals should always ensure that external sources are credible and legitimate before utilizing information in any capacity.

HR-Related Threats and Liabilities

HR-related threats and liabilities refer to events that could produce a negative impact on the organization's ability to recruit, retain, reward, and manage skilled employees who fit with the company's culture and with its professional needs. HR-related threats and liabilities can come internally, such as from high turnover rates, or they can come externally, such as from a lack of qualified applicants in an area. SWOT analyses are comprehensive tools that help to identify both internal and external threats and opportunities. In addition, they can also be used to identify strengths and weaknesses, which can then be utilized to address the more challenging aspects of established threats and opportunities. The SWOT matrix is a flexible tool that can be used to analyze small HR-related issues at the individual or departmental level, or larger issues that impact the entire organization.

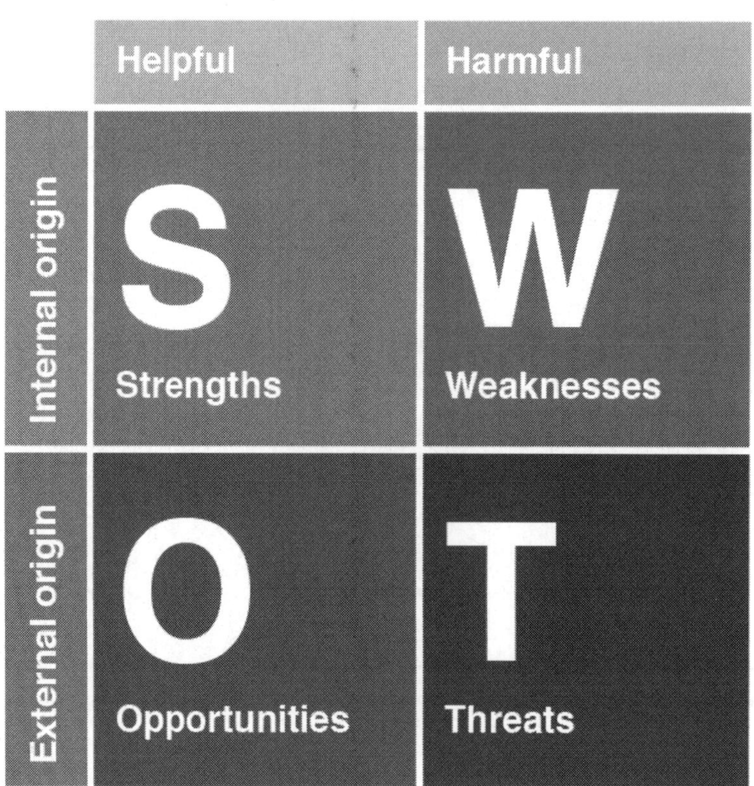

Benchmarks HR Initiatives and Outcomes Against the Organization's Competition

Benchmarking, or comparing one's initiatives and outcomes against competition, industry established standards, and industry established goals, is one way for HR professionals to determine the efficacy and value of their endeavors. It allows the organization to understand if they are creating, pricing, and delivering products or services appropriately for their targeted consumer base. Benchmarking involves developing internal metrics for key variables that can be translated to provide a comparable review against other top players in the industry. HR professionals should ensure that their benchmarking practices are relevant and comprehensive. For example, if they are trying to compare average compensation for a certain department against a competitor's, they may need to look beyond annual salary to include benefits such as 401(k) matching rates, time off, flexible work culture, and other aspects that employees could view as benefits in order to draw a true comparison between organizations.

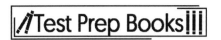

Reporting and Presentation Techniques

Data Analysis

Statistics and Measurement Concepts

While a number of software and online applications exist to make statistical methods and measurement concepts easier to use, HR professionals should maintain a basic working knowledge of these fields in order to create functional research designs and collect clean data that can be interpreted with an end goal in mind. In addition, this knowledge allows HR professionals to understand, accurately communicate, and productively apply trends derived from data sets. HR professionals should feel comfortable inputting data into software and running appropriate analyses to find the information they want. HR professionals should have a basic understanding of concepts such as means, hypothesis testing, regression analysis, and variance analysis in order to compare tests of change from baseline levels. This provides evidence that implemented initiatives are effective and can also provide insight toward certain factors which may be more effective than others.

Identifying Misleading Data

Working knowledge of statistics, measurement concepts, and other aspects of data allows the HR professional to understand when data are flawed, misleading, or should otherwise be avoided. When reviewing scholarly literature or articles in which statistics are cited, it is important to read beyond the conclusion drawn by the author. HR professionals should review sampling and methodology text within manuscripts to ensure that the sample of data collected was large enough to be statistically significant, that all influencing bias or confounders were controlled for, and that inappropriate correlations were not drawn from the data. Visual representations of data can also misconstrue the true meaning and should always be examined further. For example, if a bar chart shows a large pay gap between two sets of employees in the same department, it may appear that the organization has an unjust compensation system. However, further investigation could show that one set of employees is entry-level in experience while the other is senior.

Conducting Analyses

HR professionals must be able to apply research of best practices to practical application within their workplace and test these applications to ensure efficacy. In order to determine which research findings are critical and could make an impact within their organization, HR professionals need to examine the context in which best practices were determined. For example, a case study may correlate the implementation of a worksite wellness program with a reduction in employee health insurance claims. However, if this case study took place in an organization with 100 employees, it may not produce the same correlation in an organization with 1,000 employees. Therefore, HR professionals may need to tailor the methodology for their specific organization if this is an initiative they hope to pursue successfully. Additionally, they will need to establish a basic framework for evaluating new initiatives. Finally, HR professionals should be eager to solicit verbal or written anecdotal feedback from key stakeholders.

Objective Data Interpretation

Once data is collected, it can be challenging to maintain objectivity when interpreting it, especially if personal responsibility, time investment, or interest is at stake. Data collection is always subject to confirmation bias by the researcher, which can skew results. Additionally, data analysis does not always reflect trends that an organization hopes to see, and these findings can be indicative of ineffective processes or performance. It can be difficult to maintain an objective, rather than emotional, stance when this occurs. Additionally, negative qualitative data, especially data that come from interviews with personal opinions of stakeholders, can be difficult for interpreters to not view as a personal attack. However, it is vital to treat these contexts as learning opportunities and to reflect upon setbacks that may have occurred to cause such outcomes with nonjudgmental clarity. From there, rational and effective process and performance improvements can take place.

Impact of Technology on HR

Technology Solutions

Nowadays, organizations rely on information technology to carry out essential business functions. Some conduct the entirety of their business via the internet. These metrics can help organizations get the most out of their IT departments.

One important category analyzes the functionality of an organization's IT resources. That is, how well are IT services working? This can be measured by looking at the number of software bugs over a given period, or the average number of hours required to resolve IT issues. If there's a large volume of IT problems, or if it takes too long to fix critical IT issues, the organization must devote more resources to improving its IT functionality.

IT metrics can also consider online business activities that examine an organization's online sales presence. If a business has a website, one important metric is the number of page views. This measures the organization's reach—how many potential customers is the organization reaching through its online marketing? How many page views lead to actual purchases? How many visitors are registered on the site or subscribed to a newsletter? If the organization isn't satisfied with this number, it's time to try new online marketing strategies. The business can also look at the ratio of online sales to sales from non-internet business (for example, over the phone or in person) in order to determine where it should focus sales and marketing efforts.

Finally, as with any department, organizations must consider the cost of IT. This metric helps the organization see what portion of its financial resources is devoted to IT services, and whether this investment adds value to the organization. For example, an organization may invest on new project management software, but this software increases productivity and helps managers keep project costs low—so the cost of the software is offset by the savings it creates.

HRIS

As organizations become increasingly dependent on technology management, it is incumbent on HR professionals to identify and implement technologies that are most beneficial to their work. Human resource information systems (HRIS) are tools for managing relevant HR data, including employee information and benefits administration. It may also include an ATS that aids with recruitment by managing resumes, applicant information, open positions, etc. In the past, such information tended to be stored in discrete databases, making it difficult to integrate data and leading to frequent duplication of information. However, as the rising trend of big data analysis continues, organizations and HR departments can obtain a wealth of information from data that is properly stored and organized. Therefore, in choosing and implementing HRIS, HR professionals should consider what information is being stored at the organization, what information HR needs to know based on that data, and how data could be integrated for easier access and analysis. There is no one-size-fits-all HRIS; rather, HR professionals should consider the unique needs of their organization.

Electronic Media and Hardware Policies and Procedures

If a firm wishes to maintain competitiveness and maximize its capabilities, management should develop policies that streamline communication. These policies will allow for the freer flow of ideas and dialogue. Furthermore, the integration of electronic media will increase a firm's ability to reach out to consumers and market the company's products. Harnessing this technology can increase market share and make innovation easier.

Electronic mail, or email, is communication that occurs by exchanging digital messages. Email was developed in the early 1990s and came into widespread use by 1993. Email has become a common means of communication, particularly within a corporate environment. This mode of communication allows an individual to send messages to one or more recipients at once. Email has been enormously successful in streamlining the communication process while reducing the cost of using paper.

Many organizations currently integrate the use of social media into corporate strategies. Social media is online applications that allow users to share content. These sites have become so advantageous in marketing that companies hire designated employees to increase social media presence. Many firms presently require their employees to have social media skills, knowledge, and familiarity. Programs such as Twitter™, Facebook™, and Instagram™ have proven to be tremendously successful marketing tools used by companies to reach a broader audience. In addition, social media has revolutionized advertising by placing a growing emphasis on Internet marketing instead of traditional television ads.

As technology has increased the use of the internet, the necessity of a company website and the demand for website accessibility has grown. In order to promote equal access to websites, companies should attempt to accommodate those with cognitive, neurological, physical, visual, or auditory disabilities. In addition to disabled persons, elderly people who lack familiarity should be able to understand and navigate websites. Because the internet is an integral resource for participating in commercial activity, gaining employment, accessing health care, and finding recreational activities, equal opportunity and access to website navigation is also crucial.

Data sharing is the practice of making information accessible through public or private networks. Individuals within the network have access to the information, while those not in the network require consent for access. Data sharing usually involves varying levels of access and is generally regulated by administrators in the system.

A password is a code that is required to access restricted information. A complex password provides more security to the user and better protects sensitive information. Typically, passwords consist of letters, numbers, and symbols. This unique combination affords better protection to the user. Password sharing should be limited to those individuals who may be trusted with confidential information.

Social engineering is the act of manipulating people for the purpose of revealing sensitive information. Typically, an attacker will employ deceptive tactics to convince the target to provide information such as bank numbers, passwords, and Social Security numbers. Social engineers take advantage of a target's natural tendencies of trust. Social engineers may gain access to information by infiltrating computer systems and installing malware. Organizations should educate employees on security and the identification of untrustworthy individuals. Employees should be able to assess suspicious situations and clearly recognize red flags.

Social media is a platform where people can freely express ideas, exchange information, market goods, and advertise. Social media establishes important individual connections and can even result in locating employment. While a helpful and useful tool in many circumstances, social media may also carry unintended consequences. For example, employers often use social media to obtain personal information about a potential or current employee. Questionable social media content can influence an employer's decision to hire an individual.

Monitoring software, also known as computer surveillance software, regulates the activity performed on a certain network. If this software detects anything that may threaten the safety and security of the network, it reports the activity to an administrator. This type of software may be employed in individual or corporate networks. Typically, monitoring software checks all information flow of network traffic on the internet. Computer surveillance software is sophisticated enough to easily detect any abnormal or suspicious action in a multitude of network information.

In the field of computer security, biometrics refers to an authentication process that requires physiological proof to validate a user. Once the measure of the user's physiology is authenticated, they will be granted access to appropriate information. Biometric identification ranges from fingerprints, facial recognition, voice recognition, hand patterns, or eye patterns. The individual's biometric information is uploaded and stored in a security system that must recognize these physical characteristics to provide information access.

Managing Vendors

One of the primary benefits of a well-designed and -managed HRIS is its ability to use data to develop evidence-based solutions. Traditionally, many solutions and recommendations have been based on experience, common business practices, or long-standing assumptions that may not actually be founded on objective facts. HRIS can provide HR professionals with the analytical tools necessary to answer questions that influence policy decisions. For example, by pulling data related to employee pay, retention, and future performance, HR can formulate a more compelling case for increasing an organization's standard raise structure with recommendations that are based on concrete results from the data analysis. When there is a difficult problem, data can provide something humans sometimes cannot—an unbiased perspective. For example, an organization may be committed to diversity in its upper management, and yet it still finds that it is unable to meet diversity goals in promoting employees. Conscious and unconscious biases may be influencing who managers recommend for advancement. Standardized performance metrics that are evaluated by employee management software could produce a fair and representative list of who is qualified for a particular promotion.

Using Technology that Analyzes Data

In selecting HR technology solutions, HR professionals need to coordinate with vendors. Because salespeople are obviously not the best source for unbiased product recommendations, it is important for HR professionals to understand their organization's technology needs and do their due diligence on industry standards. Although it is important for an organization's technology capabilities to stay current, innovation can be balanced with realistic day-to-day operational needs. The time, cost, and training needed to implement a new HRIS should be weighed against the benefits it will bring to the organization. Also, cybersecurity is of vital importance in an organization's technology plan, especially when it comes to employees' sensitive personal data. While it is impossible for any vendor to guarantee absolute security, vendors should still provide security protections that are at or above industry standard, as well as provide a response plan for how to handle any software failures.

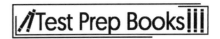

Employee Records Management

Companies should maintain maximum security while possessing the personal information of customers and employees. Each organization should utilize an apparatus that monitors and reports security breaches, notifying employees, customers, and various authorities. In addition, internal privacy policies must comply with current laws and regulations. These laws are intended to deter security breaches.

A company's internal privacy policy should address sensitive information such as addresses, telephone numbers, credit reports, medical reports, employee records, company technology, and data systems that collect personal information. An effective privacy policy explains the purposes of investigations and monitors the conduct of employees. Episodic privacy tests can be useful, particularly if management has reason to believe that employee misconduct has occurred. A company should communicate regularly with its employees about security issues and technology. Additionally, written policies must exist to protect employers from employee claims of privacy invasion. Employees should be notified of these policies and agree to all conditions. An effective privacy policy will identify and monitor employees suspected of violating protocol and procure the necessary information to review the employee's practices.

Identity theft occurs when a person wrongfully obtains and uses another individual's personal information, typically for financial gain. This form of fraud can be very damaging and is difficult to prevent. In order to commit identity theft, a perpetrator does not need a person's fingerprint. The criminal simply needs a Social Security number, credit card number, bank statements, or any piece of information that will allow access to personal documents. The expense of identity theft to the victim can be shocking, and in some cases may be in excess of $100,000. Identity theft primarily occurs in public places through methods such as "shoulder surfing." This technique involves watching over somebody's shoulder when they are using an ATM machine or rummaging through someone's garbage in search of confidential material that was not disposed of properly.

Data protection is the process of securing personal information from identity theft or other corruptive activities. Data protection involves storing important materials and can be done through a variety of means, such as file locking, disk mirroring, and database shadowing. The principal purpose of data protection is to maintain the integrity and proper storage of information. Two effective means of achieving maximum data protection while ensuring availability is to pursue data lifecycle management (DLM) and information lifecycle management (ILM), which may provide better data protection in the event of a virus or hack. A feasible data protection plan is also applicable to disaster recovery and business continuity.

Workplace monitoring is a policy that employers use in order to monitor a suspicious person and gather information. Employers may use a workplace monitoring program to discover activities that threaten the integrity and interests of the firm. Particular monitoring techniques involve wiretapping, reviewing Internet content usage, GPS tracking, checking employees' social media accounts, and interviewing other employees about suspicious activity. Management surveillance programs are easier to execute if employees are required to use company phones and computers. However, before such actions are taken by an employer, all employees should be given ample documentation of rules and regulations. This will ensure that any breach of protocol is intentional and deliberate on the part of the employee.

Statutory Reporting Requirements

The Occupational Safety and Health Act, passed in 1970, established the Occupational Safety and Health Administration (OSHA) of the federal government in 1971. This agency creates and enforces workplace safety standards. Employers who are engaged in commerce and have one or more employees must observe the regulations established by OSHA. Not only does OSHA set minimum standards, the agency ensures job training for workers in a language they can understand. Additionally, OSHA protects employees who work in substandard conditions and informs them of their rights. A critical provision of OSHA is the protection of employees who reach out to OSHA in an attempt to open an investigation of their working conditions. These employees are protected by OSHA from employer retaliation. OSHA regulations empower employees to help accomplish safety and security.

Employee Retirement Income Security Act (1974)

The Employment Retirement Income Security Act (ERISA) establishes the minimum standards for benefit plans of private, for-profit employers. It states that in order to receive tax advantages, these plans must conform to the Internal Revenue Code's requirements.

This law also established the federal agency known as the Pension Benefit Guaranty Corporation (PBGC). In return for the plans or their sponsors paying premiums to the PBGC, it guarantees payment of vested benefits up to a maximum limit to employees covered by pension plans.

Vested benefits are simply benefits from a retirement account or from a pension plan belonging to an employee that they get to keep regardless of whether they remain employed at the company. Companies have different rules regarding the number of years at which benefits vest; many are five years. Therefore, if an employee resigns after the vesting period of five years, then they can retain the benefits.

Minimum eligibility requirements were also established by ERISA. In order to participate in a plan, an employee must be at least twenty-one years of age and have completed one year of service with the company. However, company plans may be more generous concerning these minimum eligibility requirements.

ERISA established minimum vesting schedules for graded and cliff vesting. **Graded vesting** is a set schedule where employees are vested at a percentage amount less than 100 percent each year, until they accrue enough years of service to be considered 100 percent vested. **Cliff vesting** refers to employees becoming 100 percent vested after a specific number of years of service. ERISA established that employees are always 100 percent vested in their own contributions towards their retirement plans. The vesting schedules differ based on the type of retirement plan an employer is offering.

Minimum reporting standards for benefit plans were set up by ERISA. The act requires benefit plan sponsors to prepare and distribute summary plan descriptions (SPDs) to participants at least once every five years. Participants must also receive a summary annual report (SAR) that contains financial information about the plan.

Employers who fail to comply with this act may face both civil and criminal penalties. Some criminal penalties can cost companies as much as $500,000 and up to ten years in prison.

Human Resources Information Systems (HRIS)

Business technology, of which HRIS are a component, manage a great number of operations in organizations today. Business technology can refer to any software, online system, application, or other technological innovation that automates or simplifies jobs within an organization. Based on organization needs, HRIS can perform functions such as the following:

- Creating and managing online employee information systems
- Managing and updating job postings
- Updating candidate profiles over the course of the hiring process
- Managing and storing HR documents and reporting

HRIS can also store data related to the following:

- Employee productivity
- Performance
- Job satisfaction
- Benefit usage
- Historical data

These data can be analyzed through the HRIS to generate reports indicating internal trends, which can pinpoint organizational problems, needs, or successes. Due to the advent of HRIS, it is critical for business professionals to embrace new technologies and continuous learning on the job.

Job Classifications

Employee Classification

The FLSA requires employers to classify all employee positions into two categories, exempt and non-exempt, depending on the type of work the employees do, the amount of money the employees are paid, and how the employees are paid.

- **Non-exempt** positions fall directly under the FLSA regulations. These employees earn a salary of less than $23,600 per year or $455 per week. Non-exempt positions do not involve the supervision of others or the use of independent judgment; they also do not require specialized education.

- **Exempt** positions do not fall under the FLSA regulations. These employees are paid on a salary basis and spend more than 50 percent of their work time performing exempt duties. Exempt level duties fall into three main categories: executive, professional, and administrative.

    - **Executive employees** are responsible for directing the work of two or more full-time employees. Management is a key focus of their role, and they have direct input into the job status of other employees, such as hiring and firing.

    - **Professional employees** can fall into the category of learned professionals, meaning their positions require knowledge in a specific field of science or learning, such as doctors, lawyers, engineers, and accountants. Professional employees can also fall into the category of creative professionals, meaning their positions involve the invention, imagination, originality, or talent in a recognized field of artistic or creative endeavor—e.g., writing, acting, and graphic arts.

- **Administrative employees** are responsible for exercising discretion and judgment with respect to matters of significance, which can be directly related to management of the general business or in dealings with the customers of the business.

Employees and Independent Contractors

It is important for employers to be able to discern between employees and independent contractors who are performing work for them for the purpose of withholding taxes, paying overtime and on-call pay with regard to the Fair Labor Standards Act (FLSA), providing benefits, and granting legal protection to the appropriate individuals, all of which apply only to employees.

Employers are able to use independent contractors as a way to grow and reduce their workforce as needed while reducing their legal liability. There can also be a significant cost savings associated with having independent contractors complete work as they can typically be paid less than regular, full-time staff, and they do not receive healthcare benefits.

The Internal Revenue Service has developed a list of twenty factors that fall under three categories for employers to use to determine if an individual working for them is an employee or an independent contractor:

IRS 20-Factor Test
Behavioral Control
1. Instruction: A company-employee relationship could exist if the company dictates where, when, and how the employee works.
2. Training: A training relationship indicates the company has control over the type of work done by the employee.
3. Business Integration: Workers are likely to be considered employees if the success of the business depends on the work they do.
4. Personal Services: Independent contractors are free to assign work to anyone. Likewise, a company-employee relationship may dictate a particular person to carry out a specific task.
5. Assistants: An independent contractor may hire, supervise, and pay their own assistants, while a company-employee relationship may indicate that the company has control over the hiring, supervising, and paying of the worker's assistants.
Financial Control
6. Payment Method: Usually, hourly, weekly, or monthly payments indicate a company-employee relationship. Independent contractors are usually paid by commission or upon project completion.
7. Business or Travel Expenses: Employers who pay business or travel expenses for their employees are usually part of a company-employee relationship.
8. Tools and Materials: A company-employee relationship usually exists if the company provides the worker with tools and materials.
9. Investment in Facilities: Independent contractors usually invest in their own facilities, while employees for companies are usually provided facilities.
10. Profit or Loss: Workers who realize profits or losses are usually independent contractors.
Type of Relationship

11. Continuing of Relationships: An ongoing relationship between a company and a worker could indicate an employment relationship.
12. Set Hours: The implementation of a set schedule indicates that a company-employee relationship exists.
13. Full-Time: While independent contractors choose to work when and for whom they choose, employees sometimes must devote their schedules to full-time work for employees.
14. On-Site Services: If the work must be done on company property, a company-employee relationship probably exists.
15. Sequence of Work: A company-employee relationship is indicated if the worker must perform work in order of company preference and is not able to choose the sequence themselves.
16. Reports: If a worker is required to give oral or written reports to a company, this may indicate a level of control the company has over an employee.
17. Multiple Companies: Workers who provide services for multiple companies at one time are usually considered independent contractors.
18. Availability to Public: Workers who make their work available to the general public are often considered to be independent contractors.
19. Right to Discharge: Employers who have the right to discharge employees indicate a company-employee relationship.
20. Right to Terminate: Independent contractors are usually under contract to work, so they cannot terminate their employment as easily as employees.

Job Analysis Methods and Job Descriptions

After a job analysis is performed, which results in job descriptions and job specifications, a job evaluation is conducted to determine the relative worth of each job position by creating a hierarchy. This ultimately leads to the establishment of a pay structure.

- Job analysis: The process used to determine the requirements and importance of duties for a particular job
- Job descriptions: A list of general duties and responsibilities for a particular job
- Job specifications: A statement of the essential parts of a particular class of jobs. This includes a summary of the duties to be performed and responsibilities and qualifications necessary to do the job.
- Job evaluation: The ways to determine the value or worth of a job in relation to other jobs in a company

There are two main job evaluation methods: non-quantitative and quantitative.

Non-Quantitative Job Evaluation Methods

Non-quantitative job evaluation methods are also known as **whole-job methods**. The three specific examples are job ranking, paired comparison, and job classification.

Job Ranking

Job ranking involves a job-to-job comparison by developing a hierarchy of jobs from the lowest to the highest, based on each job's overall importance to the organization. This is a quick, inexpensive way for small organizations to compare one job to another.

Paired Comparison

Paired comparison is a process of comparing each job to every other job for the purpose of ranking all jobs on a scale from high to low. This is also an effective, low-cost job evaluation method for small companies.

Job Classification

Job classification involves grouping jobs into a predetermined number of grades, each of which has a class description to use for job comparisons. Benchmark jobs that fall into each class can be defined as reference points. An example of job classification put into practice is the Federal Government's use of the General Schedule classification system.

Quantitative Job Evaluation Methods

Quantitative job evaluation methods use a scaling system and provide a score that indicates how valuable one job is when compared to another job. The two specific examples are the point factor method and the factor comparison method.

Point Factor Method

The **point factor method** is less complex and most commonly used. This method uses specific, compensable factors, such as skill, responsibility, effort, working conditions, and the supervision of others, in order to evaluate the relative worth of each job. Each job receives a total point value, and then, the relative worth of all jobs within an organization can be compared.

Factor Comparison Method

The **factor comparison method** is more complex and rarely used. This method involves a ranking of each job by each selected compensable factor and then identifies dollar values for each level of each factor to develop a pay rate for an evaluated job. It is best to use this method when wages are not frequently changing and the organization uses a flat rate of pay for each job. This method can sometimes be used as part of a labor contract.

Reporting Structure

There are many types of organizational structures, each with their own HR needs. One type is a functional structure, in which positions are grouped according to similar job roles (defined by skill, expertise, or resources) in a hierarchical chain. This type of structure separates distinct job tasks and creates a clear line of job advancement. An example of this might be a retail store that has separate teams for sales and logistics; the sales team, for instance, is then further divided into sales associate, sales leader, and sales manager positions. Another type of organization structure is a divisional structure. This often applies to larger companies, and uses a department-based organizational style, where employees who work on similar projects are grouped together. The divisions may be separated by region, product type, or specific customer needs. For example, an electronics company may have different divisions for producing televisions and cellphones, even though both divisions include similar jobs like electronic engineers, product marketers, and sales representatives. A matrix structure combines elements of both functional and divisional structures. A flat structure seeks to eliminate much of the hierarchy and bureaucracy that exists in traditional companies, while a network structure outsources many key tasks to outside organizations.

External Providers

Depending on an organization's needs, contracting with an external vendor to provide HR services may be necessary. Vendors can provide external support for recruitment, benefits, compensation and classification, employee relations, and systems management. Agencies may determine that external support is required only for specific needs such as recruiting for a high-level executive, conducting a point-in-time compensation review, or investigating an employee complaint. It may be necessary, though, for an agency to contract with an outside vendor to provide full cycle services that include all elements of a particular function, or even the entire HR department.

There are pros and cons to having an external provider service an organization. Costs, subject matter expertise, consistency, fair practices, and service are all elements that should be considered when reviewing this decision. Each element should be reviewed thoroughly to ensure that the best and most appropriate decision can be made. Outsourcing specific and specialized HR functions enables the department to focus on the core responsibilities that align with the organization's goals and strategies. Some projects require trained professionals that specialize in a certain program. It may be difficult to hire an HR professional with the specific experience and expertise for one specific task. It may therefore be in the best interest to contract with an external provider for this service.

Recruitment firms can ensure that streamlined processes are established and fair practices are implemented across all hiring practices. Specialized subject matter experts in each field and position can be assigned to coordinate recruitment efforts instead of having an overall hiring specialist who has focused experience solely in recruiting. Many positions require specialized sourcing, niche marketing efforts, and even professional networking to engage prospective applicants for open employment opportunities. One such type of specialist is the benefits broker.

Benefits brokers can ensure that the best and most cost-effective benefits are offered to employees. Benefits, especially healthcare, has become an area of increased focus with specific attention to contain costs. Benefits brokers provide data and analysis to an organization that enables discussion regarding options and solutions to address the increasing costs of benefits. When an organization is considering options such as becoming self-insured or aligning with other organizations to enhance the pool for calculating premium rates, benefits brokers can provide a different perspective.

Some external HR providers focus on training. These providers enable an organization to determine the training needs of all employees, including all mandatory training, and then turn over the needs to the provider for a plan to implement and track. With mandatory training being established in some states, having accurate and updated information that shows employee training history is vital to ensure compliance if audited. An example of this is in the state of California regarding sexual harassment training. All employees must attend an interactive one-hour training within six months of hire and afterward, every two years thereafter. All supervisory employees must attend an interactive two-hour training within six months of hire or promotion and afterward, every two years thereafter. Ensuring that the training meets the legal requirements and is delivered within the required timeframes is essential for an organization operating in the state of California. Contracting with a training company that specializes in this area could be a huge benefit for an organization.

Communication Techniques

Two-Way Communication

HR professionals can develop effective and satisfactory working relationships with supervisors and HR leaders by engaging in two-way communication about project expectations, deadlines, needs, and goals. These aspects should be discussed and documented when a work assignment is first received and should take priority during the planning aspect of the project. HR professionals should expect superiors to dedicate time to this planning period. In return, HR professionals should utilize this time to ask questions about the project and bring up any questions so as to best respect the time that leadership is providing. Developing a written project proposal with leadership that outlines the timeline, milestones, resources needed, and concrete dates for deliverables can be a useful method to ensure that both HR staff members and leadership have the same expectations. Once expectations are communicated, HR professionals should make every reasonable effort to deliver results autonomously, without the need for constant leadership follow-up.

Communication Among Team Members

As an HR professional, high levels of human interaction are inherent to the nature of the work. Beyond serving employees within an organization, HR professionals can expect to work in a team within and outside of their department. Team members may be assigned by project rather than personally chosen; therefore, it is important to develop wide-ranging engagement skills that promote positive interactions. HR professionals can build their intrapersonal skills by examining their own strengths and weaknesses through analytical personality tests, and actively working to improve areas of weakness. This can be achieved by utilizing pockets of time to practice intrapersonal skills with colleagues, such as over lunch or during a meeting. Developing emotional intelligence (EI) skills also helps one recognize others' feelings and communication styles, and this information can be used to build better relationships. Maintaining a positive attitude, showing appreciation for support and tasks done well, and avoiding negative talk and behaviors also fosters team cohesiveness.

Communication Among Stakeholders and Team Members

It is also important to create teams that have members with similar professional interests and goals, in order to minimize resistance as the project progresses. However, open communication may be the most crucial component of fostering collaboration among a team. While cultivating open communication lines is a team effort, those who choose to actively model behaviors that lend to open communication are likely to become leaders within the team. Team leaders should promote an encouraging environment that allows all members and stakeholders to voice their opinions and concerns without fearing retribution. This may involve speaking with team members individually, especially if they are quieter or prefer speaking one-on-one. Finally, building relationships outside of the work setting, such as over creative social events, allows team members to get to know one another better. This can allow team members to feel more open and collaborative during the work setting.

Ways of Communication

Town hall meetings, formal gatherings for the entire company that are commonly referred to as "all-hands meetings," tend to focus on sharing information "from the top down" concerning the overall organization, and thus are not usually designed to allow feedback from employees about smaller detail issues. An **open-door policy** is used to establish a relationship where employees feel comfortable speaking directly with management about problems and suggestions. In essence, an open-door policy enables a supervisor or manager to be a "human suggestion box." There are several potential roadblocks to a successful open-door policy. In certain situations, it can be difficult to create an environment where employees feel comfortable discussing problems in person with management. In addition, depending on the problem reported, it may not be possible to maintain confidentiality. However, in the right situation, an open-door policy can help companies identify problems quickly, almost in real-time, without having to wait for a formal meeting to address an ongoing issue.

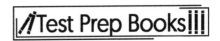

Management by Walking Around (**MBWA**), as the name suggests, involves having managers and supervisors physically get out of their offices and interact with employees in person. MBWA allows management to check on employee progress, inquire about potential issues, and gain feedback without relying on employees to "make the first move" through an open-door policy or online suggestion form. This strategy also helps prevent management from becoming isolated behind a desk and seeming distant and disinterested in employee problems.

Email makes it easy to get information to a lot of people very quickly. However, this communication method can result in employees suffering from "information overload" from too many emails, making it more likely that important information is overlooked. Also, there is a danger that confidential information may be accidentally communicated to the wrong people.

The **intranet** (internal website and computer network) has the benefit of no risk of important information being accessed by someone outside the organization. Intranets can be very effective at communicating important ongoing information about the company, such as policies and procedures. In addition, companies often store necessary workplace documentation, such as HR-related forms, on an intranet, allowing employees to access that information when they need it. However, if outside parties need information on the intranet, they cannot access it. In addition, intranet communication is often "top-down" and does not allow for feedback from employees. It is also important to note that some intranet systems are not user-friendly, and employees can be discouraged from using them.

Newsletters can provide a variety of information and have the potential to do so in an engaging, welcoming manner. However, newsletters can be labor-intensive. Since they are relatively infrequent, newsletters are not always useful for communicating urgent or immediate information. In addition, newsletters do not allow for formal two-way communication from employees, although this can be remedied by involving employees in the creation of the newsletter.

Finally, **word-of-mouth** communication can quickly spread information throughout a group of people. However, as in the children's game "Telephone," information can become muddled, misinterpreted, and downright unrecognizable as it is passed from person to person. A manager or supervisor has no control over misinterpretations and misunderstandings that can result from word-of-mouth communication.

Exchanging Organizational Information

Communicating HR Programs, Practices, and Policies to Both HR and Non-HR Employees

Organizational communication must be appropriately delivered by the sender and received by the intended recipient in order to be effective. Communicating within the HR department may be an easier task for the HR professional than communicating with outside departments, as the HR department is likely to house similar values, interests, goals, and methods of communication. The HR department, however, establishes many crucial programs, practices, and policies that affect the operations and culture of the entire organizations. Entities such as employee benefits, ethical handbooks, and company-wide events often originate in the HR department and must be shared across all departments. Effective communication strategies often employ the influence of top leadership, a reliable mode of dissemination that is favored by the majority of recipients, and evaluation practices that focus on utilizing recipient feedback to analyze the overall efficacy of the communication channel. When communicating, HR professionals should also account for informal avenues, such as break room conversation.

Helping Non-HR Managers Communicate HR Issues

Managers are excellent vectors of communication and leveraging the relationships and influence managers have with their team members can be a method of communicating organizational HR issues. In order to effectively utilize this resource, HR professionals should network with managers to build rapport and credibility. This also helps HR professionals understand what values are important to the manager; consequently, HR professionals can illustrate how HR issues impact the manager and his or her team. HR professionals should keep in mind that managers may welcome or resist serving as their team's communication channel for HR topics. It is important to make this process easy for the manager to implement, rather than seem like an additional burdensome responsibility. Finally, once this practice is established, HR professionals should remain an open and reliable liaison for the manager to return to should any HR-related questions or concerns arise.

Voicing Support for HR and Organizational Initiatives in Communications with Stakeholders

HR professionals serve as a champion for their department. Their interactions with stakeholders should reflect pride, value, and confidence in the department's work in order to maintain positive engagement from the stakeholders. Stakeholders are more likely to remain resistant if HR personnel display neutral or negative stances about their own department's initiatives. Additionally, previously engaged stakeholders may begin to lose interest or feel a loss of value. If an instance occurs where the HR professional feels they cannot support an initiative in communications with stakeholders, leadership should be notified in order to find a resolution. This may involve changing a component of the initiative, altering the communication process between the department and the stakeholder, or shifting job responsibilities in order to achieve a better fit.

Communicating with Senior HR Leaders

Effective communication with senior HR leaders allows both leadership and subordinate personnel to openly share information related to the organization's HR needs. It allows both groups to communicate in a timely manner. HR personnel should be mindful of leadership's time and commitments. This means limiting unnecessary interaction. Communication should remain concise, professional, and on topic. This can be achieved by specifically addressing why the communication is being made, what is needed from the leader, and if there is a time constraint associated with any of the needs. It can also be beneficial to recognize leadership's preferred method of communication. Finally, HR staff members should take initiative to communicate expected correspondence, such as monthly department reports or deliverables.

Listening

Listening Actively and Empathetically

Active listening pushes the listener into an engaged position. Beyond using their sense of hearing, active listeners also use their sense of sight to notice the speaker's body language. Both auditory and visual information are consciously synthesized to perceive what the speaker is trying to communicate. In addition, the listener verbally reflects the information provided by the speaker, and then asks for confirmation that the information was perceived in the way the speaker intended. Only then does the listener formulate a response. Empathetic listening includes placing oneself in the perspective of the speaker and formulating a response based on how the speaker will accept it. HR personnel often face emotionally charged conversations dealing with an employee's job or family. Utilizing active and empathetic listening skills conveys concerns for the employee and helps diffuse tense situations.

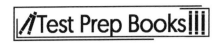

Competing Points of View

Competing points of view, when expressed respectfully, are healthy components of communication that often lead to new perspectives, collaboration, innovation, opportunities, and improvements. HR professionals should always remain open to hearing dissenting opinions and actively seek to understand the reasoning behind them. Rather than perceiving dissenting opinions as a personal attack, competing points of view should be welcomed as part of the inherent business process. They should be treated with logic and objective reasoning in order to come to a resolution. While it is impossible to satisfy every employee's opinion, HR initiatives and decisions should be made with trying to achieve the highest percentage of employee satisfaction and the best processes for company productivity in mind.

Seeking Further Information

Ambiguity can cause conflict, affect business processes, and cause distress to employees. Unfortunately, ambiguity is not always preventable due to factors that are often outside of the organization's control. In situations that are within the control of the HR professional, active listening practices are an important component of clear communication. The listener may need to directly state that they are confused and ask specific questions that result in a clear "Yes" or "No" answer. The listener may also need to observe the speaker's body language to determine whether the content is purposely being presented with ambiguity. However, speculation is never a good route to take to determine answers. When possible, directly asking the speaker to clarify is most likely to result in a positive result.

Addressing Stakeholder Communications

Stakeholders are considered as such because they are directly impacted by the actions of the HR department. Therefore, they are highly valuable to the efficacy of HR initiatives. Comments from them should be prioritized. Stakeholder communications can take place in person, in meetings as a group, through email, or through social media. There may not always be time to respond to stakeholder questions, especially if they are unanticipated and come up in person. In these instances, it is important for HR professionals to clearly indicate that they will need to source more information and follow up with the stakeholders. Additionally, it is important to always have the best method of contact information for each stakeholder on hand.

Received Communications

When HR professionals receive communication, they should be able to accurately identify the reason behind it. While motives for a message may not be directly stated, HR professionals can use contextual understanding. However, HR professionals should form this understanding based on objective logic, without making assumptions that are not rooted in fact. When motives for a message cannot be objectively determined, the HR professional should feel confident responding in a way that asks clarifying questions and dispels any ambiguity. Otherwise, assumptions about intention within a message can cause muddled decision-making that can have widespread ramifications.

Soliciting Feedback from Senior Leaders

Soliciting feedback is a crucial component of program evaluation, guiding and sustaining initiatives, and providing valuable customer service. HR professionals serve all units of an organization. Therefore, they should solicit feedback from leadership in all areas, keeping in mind that different leaders may have various needs and values. Learning organizational needs through the lens of each department can increase employee engagement, provide the value that leadership are asking for, and propel operations.

HR professionals can solicit feedback from leadership through online evaluation surveys, in-person meetings, and group meetings. They should ask leadership what initiatives are going well and why, and what areas need more support. HR professionals should always leave open communication channels for leadership to propose new projects and ideas. These endeavors highlight the value of a company's HR department.

Practice Questions

1. Which best describes corporate social responsibility?

   a. Corporate social responsibility is a policy mandated by the government to coerce corporations to improve their communities.

   b. Corporate social responsibility refers to the responsibility that corporations have toward shareholders.

   c. Corporate social responsibility is an issue of ethics, pursued by corporations that see the health of their business as contingent upon the health of their community.

   d. Corporate social responsibility refers to the social climate of the organization and the policies created to sustain the strength of that climate.

2. CSR can be evaluated on which three P's of the "triple bottom line"?

   a. People, prizes, and proxy

   b. Planet, profit, and projects

   c. People, profit, and prizes

   d. People, planet, and profit

3. What's the purpose of a vision statement?

   a. A vision statement is a memo drafted by management that articulates that if company policy is breached, there will be severe consequences.

   b. A vision statement is a succinct explanation of how an organization plans to deliver quality products/services.

   c. A vision statement is a lengthy and detailed speech given by a CEO to shareholders and other investors.

   d. A vision statement is a short address that low-level employees give to management.

4. In regard to corporate social responsibility, the most common ways for a corporation to assimilate into a community includes all of the following EXCEPT?

   a. The most common way for a corporation to pursue social responsibility is to establish alliances with respected members of the community and outside organizations.

   b. The most common way for a corporation to pursue social responsibility is to deliver inexpensive goods and services for the community.

   c. The most common way for a corporation to pursue social responsibility is hiring as many locals as possible.

   d. The most common way for a corporation to pursue social responsibility is by maximizing their profits despite any consequences to the surrounding environment.

5. What's the primary purpose of organizational branding?

I. The intent of organizational branding is letting customers know when they walk into a store.
II. One purpose of organizational branding is to establish a distinctive image for consumers to automatically recognize.
III. Organizational branding allows entities to create a perception of the values and ethics for which it stands.
IV. Organizational branding focuses on promoting the benefits of the company in order to appeal to a target audience.

a. I, II, and IV only
b. I, III, and IV only
c. II and III only
d. I, II and III only

6. What is the main purpose of a cost-benefit analysis?

a. When evaluating a policy or program, a cost-benefit analysis empirically tests its efficacy to ensure that resources aren't squandered.
b. Cost-benefit analyses are rarely conducted because they are expensive and unreliable.
c. When evaluating a policy or program, a cost-benefit analysis is conducted that rationally tests its efficacy to ensure that resources aren't squandered. However, because cost-benefit analyses are antiquated, management typically decides on the policy or program based on its organizational popularity.
d. A cost-benefit analysis is the empirical testing of a policy or program. However, management is typically disdainful of them because of a belief that the testers are inherently biased.

7. What are business metrics?

a. Business metrics are quantifiable measures that describe the productive capacity of a policy, program, or product.
b. Business metrics are informal activities that management occasionally conducts in order to discover the feasibility of a policy, program, or product.
c. Business metrics are typically utilized to weed out underperforming employees.
d. Business metrics are meetings with representatives from each department to voice concerns and establish harmonious, firm-wide standards and practices.

8. All of the following are part of the core meaning of competitive advantage EXCEPT?

a. Competitive advantage is the practice of constantly attempting to increase market share by exploiting advantages.
b. By constantly developing a labor force and technology, competitive advantage is pursued by all corporations in order to edge out competitors in the market.
c. It's mandatory that organizations pursue policies of competitive advantage because they all want to maximize output and increase market share.
d. Competitive advantage is a type of benefit that customers believe they could not get anywhere else.

Differential Advantage = benefits that are relevant to the purchasing decision / competitors can't duplicate

* competitive advantage = a condition or circumstance that puts a company in a favorable or superior business position

9. Which of the following statements LEAST describes corporate governance?
   a. Corporate governance is the established policies, rules, and standards that organizations follow in order to fulfill its vision and goal as a for-profit entity and a stakeholder in the broader community.
   b. Public policy influences corporate governance, i.e. the Sarbanes-Oxley Act.
   c. Corporate governance addresses rules, practices, and institutions that protect and manage ecosystems in relation to the environment.
   d. Corporate governance is necessary to establish an organization's self-image and can be used as an instrument to restore institutional trust.

10. Which of the following is true about corporate restructuring?
   a. Corporate restructuring is intended to make a firm more competitive.
   b. Corporate restructuring is a change in operations, legal code, or ownership inside of a firm.
   c. Corporate restructuring is only a euphemism for cutting labor and lowering wages.
   d. The principal purpose of corporate restructuring is to increase profits for senior executives.

11. Which of the following best describes enterprise risk management (ERM)?
   a. Enterprise risk management is when each department crafts its own policies and procedures for handling issues of risk and loss.
   b. Enterprise risk management policies are crafted only by senior executives and then handed down to all departments to follow.
   c. Enterprise risk management is the process of establishing a broad but comprehensive protocol for handling issues of risk and loss.
   d. Enterprise risk management is when a company participates in a high-risk situation in order to maximize profits for the good of the company.

12. All of the following is true about offshoring EXCEPT?
   a. Offshoring is typically done to reduce the costs of business.
   b. Offshoring involves shifting business operations to a country where business can be conducted at lower costs.
   c. The only beneficiary of offshoring is the company itself.
   d. Offshoring is one aspect of corporate restructuring that permits a company to remain competitive.

13. All of the following is necessary for an organization to pay attention to the legislative and regulatory environment EXCEPT?
   a. To anticipate changes and craft corporate governance policies that address new regulations and legislation.
   b. To engage in lobbying efforts in order to fight proposed changes that could be damaging to the corporation.
   c. To modify and make new legislative and regulatory changes more palatable.
   d. To examine competitors and match their own legislation to that of other corporations.

14. Which definition most accurately explains a whistle-blower?
   a. A whistle-blower is a person who reports any unethical information about an organization.
   b. A whistle-blower is a person hired by an organization to cover up illicit or unethical activity.
   c. A whistle-blower is a person who reports or publicizes any illegal or unethical information about the institution. Whistle-blower status is only granted when the organization is private.
   d. A whistle-blower reports or publicizes any illegal or unethical information about the institution. Whistle-blower status is only granted when the organization is public.

15. Which of the following is NOT a key component of a business plan?
   a. Annual goals
   b. Projected growth targets
   c. Net income expectations
   d. Bonuses for executives

16. A stakeholder is any actor that affects or can be affected by a business but doesn't own property of the business. Which of following groups of people are NOT stakeholders?
   a. Employees
   b. Surrounding businesses
   c. Shareholders
   d. The local community

17. Which of the following best describes mergers and acquisitions (M&A)?
   a. Mergers occur temporarily in order to consolidate resources and beat out a competitor; acquisitions occur permanently.
   b. Mergers occur when one company purchases another without a new company being formed. Acquisitions occur when two companies combine to form a new one.
   c. Mergers occur when two companies combine to form a new one. Acquisitions occur when one company purchases another without a new company being formed.
   d. Mergers and acquisitions often occur temporarily in order to consolidate resources and beat out a competitor; then the actions are rescinded and the entities disband.

18. When performing a cost-benefit analysis of a proposed project, what is a project worker's salary an example of?
   a. A stakeholder
   b. A cost
   c. A benefit
   d. A dependent variable

19. Each fiscal quarter within a fiscal year is an example of which of the following?
   a. Benchmarking
   b. A milestone
   c. Calendar divides
   d. Bonus assessment period

20. Myra and Angela are two HR professionals who work in the same organization. Recently, Myra successfully implemented a sustainability initiative with the marketing department, where she helped them reduce the amount of paper they use. This led to saved paper, printing, and labor costs as well as reduced physical waste. Angela would like to try this initiative with the finance department, which is welcome to this idea. How can Angela begin to allocate resources for this project?
   a. Copy Myra's initiative as closely as possible, right down to the budget and timeline.
   b. Use her best guess to document what she believes the finance department will need in order to reduce their paper waste, and provide a written copy to the manager.
   c. Set up a meeting with Myra to discuss how she allocated resources and what went successfully, as well as what did not go successfully, and use this data to plan.
   d. Ask the HR intern to devote all of his time to her initiative .

21. Michael leads an HR department at a federal agency. He is in the planning stage for the new fiscal year and is thrilled that he has created initiatives that are highly detailed and comprehensive and use the resources of contracts his agency currently has in place. He is very attached to the outcomes of these initiatives. However, a presidential election is taking place in one month that will likely affect the contracts that are awarded to his agency. What can Michael do to protect his new fiscal year plans?

a. Ensure that there is leftover money from the previous fiscal year to serve as a cushion should he not receive expected contracts
b. Create backup plans for all of the contracts that may be affected, while calmly accepting that some changes may be unanticipated and out of his control
c. Nothing, he has already distributed them to employees and archived them on the organization's servers
d. Find a new job

22. Larry manages three HR employees. Jane is in charge of compensation and benefit tasks, Ira is in charge of risk management tasks, and Samir is in charge of recruitment and hiring. Samir has an illness that takes him out of the office for six weeks, and during this time, all recruitment and hiring processes freeze. This majorly impacts two other departments that were waiting on new employees to begin. How could this situation have best been prevented?

a. Larry should have cross-trained his three employees to fill in for each other should emergencies come up.
b. Samir should have worked remotely to handle the candidates needed by the other two departments.
c. Larry should have filled in for Samir's role for the entire duration of his absence.
d. Ira should have analyzed Samir's workday operations to see if anything at work caused his illness.

23. What is the most crucial aspect of successfully implementing organizational change?

a. Work ethic
b. Leadership buy-in
c. Highly compensated employees
d. Terminating employees who do not agree

24. An employee sees a close colleague change numbers in an accounting spreadsheet to reflect incorrect values. The employee feels uncomfortable reporting the colleague, due to their friendship and close working relationship. However, the employee feels very concerned about the situation. What is one feasible resource that could help this employee in a situation like this?

a. An anonymous and confidential HR hotline
b. A close relationship with a superior
c. An in-house coffee shop where the employee can go with the colleague to discuss their feelings about the situation
d. Regular communication training sessions

25. What is the best way for HR leaders to communicate acceptable and ethical behaviors in the workplace?

a. Provide written protocols about what constitutes as ethical and unethical behavior
b. Relay that employees are continuously monitored with in-house cameras, so they should be especially mindful of their work behavior
c. Model acceptable and ethical behavior themselves, as much as possible
d. Tell employees at their new hire orientation

26. The CEO of a company holds bi-weekly meetings with his entire organization to relay new information about company performance, trends, and personal opinions relating to the industry. What is this an example of?

a. Transparency
b. Overshare
c. Validation
d. Process control

27. Where should an employee first encounter an organization's ethical standards and policies?

a. At the new hire orientation
b. During the first interview
c. In the job posting for his or her role
d. By reading a company press release

28. The vice-president of an organization has noticed that a particular employee, Ben, has been working extremely hard and has made a positive impression on a large majority of the organization's leadership. The vice-president meets with Ben and asks him about his work. Ben shares all of the accomplishments that his team has achieved in the last quarter. What is Ben displaying during this meeting?

a. Ego
b. Individualistic behavior
c. Team-oriented culture
d. Humility

29. During a project meeting, Mary creates a table that includes a detailed description of every task needed for the project, a deliverable date for each task, and the owner of each task. Each member is able to access and update the table with status updates. What is Mary helping her team do?

a. Helping each member feel accountable
b. Micromanaging
c. Modeling ethical behavior
d. Collecting data

30. Soliciting feedback from stakeholders is an important part of which of the following process stages?

a. Evaluation
b. Control
c. Testing
d. Documentation

31. Which of the following is an exception to the concept of employment-at-will?

a. An employee who decides to willingly sever the employment relationship
b. An employee who is terminated for whistleblowing or for reporting unlawful conduct by the employer
c. An employer who lets an employee go who does not have an employment contract
d. An employee who is fired for willful misconduct

32. A truck driver kills a family's small child in an accident, and it is later uncovered that the truck driver lied on his employment application, had a history of unsafe driving, and had his license revoked twice. The employer was ultimately held responsible by the family's attorney for which of the following?

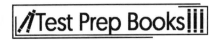

a. Negligent retention
b. Constructive discharge
c. Negligent hiring
d. Defamation

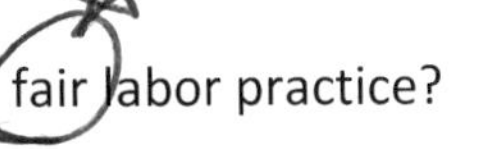

33. Which of the following activities is considered to be a fair labor practice?

a. Hot cargo agreement
b. Jurisdictional strike
c. Secondary boycott
d. Sympathy strike

34. Which of the following employees would not be eligible to vote in an upcoming union election?

a. An employee who is temporarily laid off
b. An employee who is out sick with the flu
c. An employee who is out on military leave right before the election
d. A staff member who is out of the office on a medical leave of absence and who will not be returning to work

35. Under the Taft-Hartley Act, which of the following is illegal?

a. Creating a company-sponsored labor union
b. An employee deciding to contribute to a charity instead of paying union dues, due to their religious objection
c. An employer filing an unfair labor practice charge against a union
d. A union representing nonunion employees in the bargaining unit

36. Which of the following is a true statement regarding a modified duty assignment?

a. A modified duty assignment is a temporary reassignment that seeks to accommodate employees who are recovering from illness or injury.
b. A modified duty assignment is a permanent arrangement of work to accommodate employees who are injured.
c. In order to make more money, a modified duty assignment is more work given to employees who ask for it.
d. Injured employees must accept a modified duty assignment and be examined by a licensed physician to be cleared for the assignment.

37. Which of the following most accurately describes a procurement policy?

a. A procurement policy is a strategy that employers use to find the most qualified employees.
b. A procurement policy is an organization's strategy to obtain and secure goods and services in an orderly and beneficial way to minimize cost and maximize savings.
c. A procurement policy is an analysis of an organization's inventory in order to determine what supplies are needed.
d. A procurement policy is any action that an organization takes to find a new location.

38. What is a hazard communication program, and is it legally binding?

a. A hazard communication program is a guideline that gives employers the option to inform employees when they are working with hazardous materials and is not legally binding.

b. A hazard communication program is a mandate from OSHA that requires employers to inform employees when they are working with hazardous materials and the nature of each material and is legally binding.

c. A hazard communication program is an evacuation procedure that is intended for emergencies and is legally binding.

d. A hazard communication program is an educational training program that OSHA offers to employers regarding dangerous chemicals and is not legally binding.

39. To reduce operating costs, a company has decided to maintain its domestic headquarters but open an overseas manufacturing plant. What is the best word to describe this move?

a. Outsourcing

b. Downsizing

c. Offshoring

d. Globalizing

40. An organization is using a legacy HRIS because long-standing employees are comfortable with the software and feel it continues to meet their data management needs. However, several new employees are having difficulty using the outdated user interface and are pushing to adopt an entirely new platform. What is a good solution for this situation?

a. Contract with a vendor that offers interface layer technology to develop a new user interface while maintaining the existing system.

b. Get rid of the old system and invest in the latest HRIS before the current software becomes even more outdated than it already is.

c. Reassign the new employees to positions that already have more cutting-edge software in place.

d. Create an organization-wide site where employees can submit anonymous feedback about using the current HRIS.

41. What part of a SWOT analysis evaluates internal factors that affect an organization's performance?

a. Strengths and weaknesses

b. Sources and ways

c. Output and take-in

d. Opportunities and threats

42. What does "benchmarking" refer to in an HR context?

a. Putting an employee "on the bench" or on the sidelines due to past performance

b. Linking salary increases to performance metrics

c. Identifying and setting goals relative to other organizations' performance

d. Adhering to government regulations and other industry guidance

43. What factors does a PESTLE analysis take into consideration?

a. People, projects, and payments within an organization

b. Political, economic, social, technological, legal, and environmental trends that influence the organization

c. People, engagement, sustainability, time, limitations, and expectations in relation to a specific project

d. The most proximal direct competitor

44. What is the purpose of a root cause analysis?
    a. To determine the foundation-level reason as to why an overarching issue is occurring
    b. To determine the exact employee that caused an error during a process
    c. To determine the best source of external funding
    d. To determine how to allocate fixed funds within an organization

45. What are two popular search tools to find peer-reviewed, evidence-based research?
    a. CNN and FOX
    b. Medline and Yahoo News
    c. Google Scholar and PubMed
    d. People Quest and People Soft

46. Meeting, learning from, and socializing with colleagues within and outside of one's organization is known as which of the following practices?
    a. Networking
    b. Achieving work-life balance
    c. Formal education
    d. Fraternizing

47. Lisa is an HR generalist that is posting a job online. She is proud of her company's benefits system and wants to highlight some of them in the posting. What types of benefits could she include in the job posting?
    a. Company-sponsored worksite wellness program, 401(k) matching up to 5%, and an annual sponsored mindfulness retreat
    b. Job tasks, including the amount of time spent sitting each day
    c. Number of direct reports for the position
    d. An exact salary number

48. During new hire orientation, Joe wants to illustrate the company culture to new employees. What are some things he could share with them to show the organization's culture?
    a. Share that employees can choose to work remotely one day per week, that leadership sits with employees in an open workspace, and the last Friday of each month is used to celebrate an employee's personal heritage
    b. Share that new equipment will be delivered at the end of the month, and that he will follow up with each employee on assignment
    c. Share his personal career story, beginning from choosing a major in college
    d. Enroll employees in a required CPR/AED course

1st take 72.9%
13 wrong

Answer Explanations

1. C: Corporate social responsibility is an ethical standard pursued by corporations that see the health of their business as contingent upon the health of their community. This ethical issue emphasizes becoming a part of the community and its social fabric. Corporate social responsibility can engender controversy by suggesting that a business has an obligation greater than merely supplying goods and services at a low cost.

2. D: CSR can be evaluated by people, planet, and profit. *People* refers to the organization's treatment of their employees as well as members of the community. *Planet* refers to the impact the organization has on the environment. *Profit* refers to the organization's overall contribution to economic growth. Choices *A*, *B*, and *C* are all incorrect.

3. B: A vision statement is a concise statement that reflects organizational confidence and long-term aspirations about how the firm will achieve more than just economic success. Some questions that may be answered in a vision statement include: How does this firm fit into the marketplace? How would it positively change the world? Institutionally, how does the company plan to deliver their product or service cheaper and more efficiently than competitors? Ultimately, vision statements serve the purpose of boosting trust, confidence, and an image that the firm is engaging in a task larger than itself.

4. D: Maximizing profits despite any consequences to the surrounding environment is not part of social responsibility. When practicing corporate social responsibility, there are several ways an organization can engage the community. First, a firm can establish alliances with influential members of the community or a respected local organization. Secondly, a firm can deliver on its promise of delivering low-cost goods and services to the community. Lastly, as one tenet of corporate responsibility is improving the quality of life in a community, it should hire as many locals as possible.

5. D: Organizational branding can serve multiple purposes. One is creating a distinctive logo that is easily identifiable to consumers. Furthermore, organizational branding represents an opportunity to establish a perception of values and ethics that consumers understand when they see the logo. The famous logo for the Michelin Corporation is a jovial tire man, which articulates friendly service and exactly what the firm sells. The numeral IV is not part of branding, but more of a characteristic of marketing.

6. A: A cost-benefit analysis is an objective empirical study of the precise effects of a specific policy or plan. Cost-benefit analyses are critically important because they indicate if a policy or plan will save resources or squander them. If the costs outweigh the benefits, then an action isn't financially sensible. But if the analysis indicates that benefits will outweigh costs, then the policy can be pursued with confidence.

7. A: Business metrics are quantifiable ways to assess and measure the efficacy of specific policies, programs, or products. Similar to cost-benefit analysis, these metrics are objective and inform the firm whether an action should proceed. Metrics should be used when speaking to consumers and investors in order to establish trust and confidence.

8. D: A type of benefit that customers believe they could not obtain anywhere else is an example of differential advantage, not competitive advantage. Competitive advantage is the strategy of maintaining maximum competitiveness by pursuing policies and programs that increase one's advantage. Examples of competitive advantage are implementing new technology, offshoring to lower business costs, and shedding underperforming or unnecessary laborers.

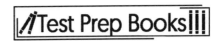

9. C: Rules, practices, and institutions that address ecosystems in relation to the environment are known as environmental governance. Corporate governance refers to the policies and institutional code that a firm establishes in order to fulfill its role as a for-profit entity and an integral stakeholder in the community. Of course, firms are not the only actors that shape its governance laws—public policy has a salient role. The Sarbanes-Oxley Act mandated new protocol that senior executives must follow in order to increase transparency and accountability. Moreover, corporate governance can serve as a valuable tool for cultivating a firm's self-image.

10. B: Corporate restructuring is a broad term to describe a change in a firm's operations, legal code, or ownership to make it more competitive by increasing productive potential and lowering costs. One aspect of corporate restructuring is offshoring. Offshoring—moving the physical operations of a firm to a different country—is done in order to lower business costs while maintaining maximum competitiveness.

11. C: Enterprise risk management (ERM) are comprehensive policies and procedures that dictate how an organization handles risk and loss. The purpose of ERM is to coordinate and create a harmony of responses to problems facing an organization. ERMs lead to greater levels of stability and structure.

12. C: Offshoring can have many positive effects that transcend the corporation. Offshoring reduces the costs of business, which leads to lower prices for consumers. Lowering business costs doesn't just lead to lower prices—it also frees up revenue to participate in philanthropic activity.

13. D: Choice *D* mimics the wording of the question, but the explanation is irrelevant. It's imperative that firms anticipate potential changes in public policy because they must adjust. The success of this adjustment will depend upon institutional preparedness. Furthermore, if anticipated changes are expected to be damaging, a firm will want to engage in lobbying efforts to modify and amend the policies.

14. A: A whistle-blower reports or publicizes any illegal or unethical information about an organization or industry. An example of a whistle-blower is former tobacco industry official Jeffrey Wigand, who confessed in a televised interview that the tobacco industry was intentionally packing cigarettes with addictive levels of nicotine. Whistle-blowers are generally perceived as villains to institutions, while others believe they risk their livelihood for a just cause. Whistleblowers can operate in public or private institutions.

15. D: A business plan has a variety of different projections. Some of these projections are annual goals, projected growth targets, and net income expectations. However, bonuses for executives aren't calculated in a business plan, which are intended to increase the firm's profitability and productivity.

16. C: Although shareholders can be affected by a business, they are not stakeholders because they have stock ownership. Stakeholders have other interests in a business besides profitability. Employees, surrounding businesses, and the local community all have a stake in the financial state of a business, but their concerns transcend the appreciation of its stock.

17. C: Mergers occur when two companies combine to form a new one. Acquisitions occur when one company purchases another without forming a new company. One notable merger occurred in 1999, when Exxon and Mobile merged to form ExxonMobil. It can be helpful to think of mergers as consolidations.

18. B: The worker's compensation is calculated as one of the costs needed to get the project done. Without paying the worker, he or she cannot be used as a resource on the project. The worker is not necessarily a stakeholder. The worker's salary is a benefit to the worker directly in return for his or her work, but it is not considered a benefit for the purpose of a cost-benefit analysis. The worker's pay is also fixed as a salary and is not considered a dependent variable for the purpose of the analysis.

19. B: Milestones are progressive periods by which certain business activities are expected to be completed.

20. C: When implementing a new initiative, HR professionals can examine internal data from similar projects to help make their planning stage as useful and accurate as possible before beginning implementation. However, Angela should not copy Myra's initiative directly, as she is working with a different team that has different needs.

21. B: Even with the most diligent planning, HR leaders should expect the unexpected and never be too emotionally attached to outcomes. Michael should realize that all baseline plans are fluid and manage his expectations accordingly, while also preparing contingency plans for his operations. Most federal funds cannot roll over from fiscal years, and simply communicating information does not set them in stone.

22. A: Larry should have cross-trained his employees to fill in for one another in the case of emergencies. This allows normal business operations to continue, rather than halt, if an employee is absent. Samir should not have to work remotely when ill, and as a team leader, Larry should not be expected to step in and fulfill Samir's entire full-time job. Analyzing Samir's workday for causes of the illness is unnecessary unless Samir requests it.

23. B: Leadership buy-in promotes top-down change; without leaders in the company supporting new initiatives, it is highly unlikely that subordinate employees will embrace change. They are more likely to resist if they feel those in leadership positions do not find the change valuable.

24. A: An anonymous and confidential hotline can help employees report potentially unethical behaviors and feel less discomfort than if they had to do so publicly.

25. C: Modeling ethical behavior is the most effective way to show employees what is acceptable in the workplace. The other methods listed can help, but they may not be very effective on their own.

26. A: Transparency allows employees to know what is going on in most, if not all, aspects of the organization as it relates to their job. High transparency is associated with employees who feel valued, validated, and report high morale.

27. C: The job posting is the first place to share the company's mission, vision, and ethical standards. This attracts candidates with similar values to apply. Ethical standards should be reviewed again during the interview process and new hire orientation to ensure good fit and promote the values.

28. C: Rather than speaking about all of his hard work and contributions, Ben chose to share his team's accomplishments without singling anyone out. This is a display of strong team-oriented culture in the workplace.

29. A: Mary is providing clear, visible expectations of project tasks and completion dates. By sharing who is assigned to each task, it provides a sense of transparency and ownership. Together, these help individual members feel accountable for the role they play on the project.

30. A: Feedback is an important part of the evaluation stage, which examines if processes were implemented smoothly, effectively, and provided value.

31. B: An employee who is terminated for whistleblowing or for reporting unlawful conduct by the employer is an exception to the concept of employment-at-will, since these activities are protected under the law.

32. C: The employer was ultimately held responsible for negligent hiring. In this example, the employer should have known that the employee posed a risk to other employees or to customers. If the employer had completed a thorough background check, they would have checked the employee's past driving record (since it was relevant to his position).

33. D: A sympathy strike is considered to be a fair labor practice. Choice *A*, hot cargo agreements, Choice *B*, jurisdictional strikes, and Choice *C*, secondary boycotts, are all considered to be unfair labor practices.

34. D: An employee who is out of the office on a medical leave of absence and who will not be returning to work would not be eligible to vote in an upcoming union election. An employee who is temporarily laid off, an employee who is out sick with the flu, and an employee who is out on military leave right before the election would all be eligible to vote in an upcoming union election.

35. A: Under the Taft-Hartley Act, creating a company-sponsored labor union is illegal.

36. A: A modified duty assignment is a temporary arrangement that offers injured or sick employees the option to work through their condition at a reduced capacity. These assignments are also dubbed "light work." Under many circumstances, modified duty is beneficial to both employers and employees, but employees do have the right to deny an employer's request if they are unable to perform the task.

37. B: Procurement policies are regulations that allow an organization to obtain and secure goods and services in an orderly and beneficial way to minimize cost and maximize savings. The size of an organization needs to be carefully considered when crafting a procurement policy, but the intent is to maximize productivity and minimize expenses. Typically, large organizations command greater bargaining power than smaller organizations.

38. B: A hazard communication program is a federal law mandated by OSHA that requires employers to inform employees when they are working with hazardous materials and the nature of such materials. It stipulates that dangerous health and noxious physical effects must be communicated to employees before they begin a specific job. The provision of OSHA that deals with hazard communication is the Hazard Communication Standard (HCS). In addition to the HCS, all organizations containing hazardous chemicals must provide hazardous material training to employees, access to material safety data sheets (MSDS), and proper labeling of containers. Hazard communication is legally binding.

39. C: Offshoring. Offshoring refers to the relocation of some or all of an organization's processes to an international location, either internally or through third-party vendors. Choice *A* is not correct because outsourcing refers to moving an organization's processes outside the company by contracting third-party vendors; outsourcing can take place either domestically or internationally. Outsourcing and offshoring may often coincide, but they are not necessarily the same thing. Choice *B* is also incorrect; an organization downsizes when it reduces its operations and eliminates previously staffed positions. Finally, Choice *D* is incorrect because globalizing is a very broad term for engaging in operations on an international scale; it is not the best term to describe this specific situation.

40. A: Contract with a vendor that offers interface layer technology to develop a new user interface while maintaining the existing system. Because the main issue is the user interface—that is, the part of the software that employees use to access and manage the data—interface layer technology can help to extend the usefulness of the system. Although it is important to stay on top of technology developments, it is impractical and costly to make major system changes that may not be necessary.

41. A: Strengths and weaknesses. The acronym SWOT stands for strengths, weaknesses, opportunities, and threats. The strengths and weaknesses a SWOT analysis reveals are internal factors that put the organization at an advantage or disadvantage compared to other organizations in the industry. Opportunities and threats are external factors that can positively or negatively influence an organization's performance.

42. C: Identifying and setting goals relative to other organizations' performance. Benchmarking involves doing environmental scanning, locating leaders in the field, and determining what those organizations have done to achieve success. Through benchmarking, an organization can learn from others' success in setting and reaching performance goals.

43. B: The acronym in PESTLE stands for political, economic, social, technological, legal, and environmental. This refers to categorized trends that influence the organization and can be used to anticipate potential opportunities and risks in a variety of areas.

44. A: A root cause analysis is a systematic review of a larger issue that is broken down into smaller issues in order to determine the single "root cause" behind the larger issue. The aim of the root cause analysis is to resolve the root cause in order to have a positive domino effect on larger issues.

45. C: Google Scholar pulls all scholarly research through Google's search engine, and PubMed provides access to a wide range of legitimate medical, health, and life (including HR topics) research.

46. A: Networking refers to interacting with others who have knowledge and expertise that can provide personal and professional growth. This action does not relate to work-life balance and is not a type of formal education. It is also a positive experience, whereas fraternizing normally has a negative connotation.

47. A: These are all unique benefits that would seem attractive to most employees. While job tasks and reports could be listed on the job posting, they do not fall under benefits. Salary is considered compensation and not an exact benefit; in addition, an exact salary is not usually posted in a job description.

48. A: These behaviors describe the attitudes, beliefs, and values that dictate the company's work days. The other options are relevant to job duties or could be ways to connect with the employees but do not reflect the overall company culture.

Recruitment and Selection

Laws and Regulations Related to Recruitment and Selection

There are many federal laws to consider when planning for new hires. One is the Civil Rights Act of 1964—specifically, Title VII, which prohibits employers from discriminating against employees on the basis of sex, race, color, national original, and religion. This act led to the creation of the Equal Employment Opportunity Commission (EEOC), which enforces and oversees laws against workplace discrimination. The definition of workplace discrimination has since been expanded to include protection from discrimination based on an employee's disability, children, sexual orientation, gender identity, genetic information, and reporting discriminatory practices. Title VII generally applies to employers with fifteen or more employees.

HR should keep EEOC rules in mind when crafting job descriptions and advertisements. For example, a job posting should not say that the company is only looking for workers in a specific age range (such as, "Only graduates from after 1999 should apply") or gender. These rules also need to be followed during all hiring procedures, including job interviews and background checks. Interviewers should not ask any questions related to the protected identities listed above. For example, questions like, "Do you have children?" or "Would you prioritize your children above your job duties?" are prohibited discriminatory questions. The interviewer should consider what skills and capabilities are actually important, and rephrase the question accordingly—perhaps something like, "How do you prioritize competing obligations?" or "Are you able to work a flexible schedule?" This is also true when checking references and contacting past employers. For example, the interviewer would not be able to ask questions such as, "Can you describe the employee's medical history?" or "Did the employ take many sick days or have any health problems that made them unable to work?" because these questions would be discriminating based on disability. Better questions might be, "Did the employee have good attendance?" or "Did the employee complete all essential job tasks?"

In 1978, the EEOC along with the Department of Labor, Department of Justice, and U.S. Civil Service Commission adopted the Uniform Guidelines on Employee Selection Procedures (UGESP) to provide standards on what constitutes discriminatory hiring practices. UGESP established the four-fifths rule, which states that if the selection rate for any race, sex, or ethnic group is less than four-fifths of the selection rate for the group with the highest selection rate, the hiring practice is generally considered discriminatory. For example, from a pool of applicants, a company hires 8 percent of the men who applied, but only 2 percent of the women who applied. In this case, the selection rate for women is only 25 percent of the selection rate for men—less than four-fifths (or 80 percent). This would be deemed discriminatory hiring.

Another relevant law is the Fair Labor Standard Act of 1938 (FLSA), which establishes standards for a minimum wage, overtime pay, recordkeeping, and child labor standards. There are some exemptions to FLSA (for example, many tip-based professions such as food service), but it generally covers employers with at least $500,000 of business in a year. There are also other laws related to pay for specific professions. The Walsh-Healey Public Contracts Act of 1936 establishes labor rights for U.S. government contracts, and it applies to any contracts exceeding $10,000 for goods. Like the FLSA, it sets standards for overtime pay and child labor, prohibiting the employment of those under the age of 16. It sets a separate minimum wage using the prevailing wage, as determined by state departments of labor. The prevailing wage is defined as the standard hourly wage, overtime, and benefits paid to the majority of workers in a given area. Another contract act is the McNamara-O'Hara Service Contract Act of 1965 (SCA), which applies to contractors and subcontractors working on service contracts exceeding $2,500. Those contractors or subcontractors are also required to pay service employees no less than the prevailing wage. The Department of Labor oversees compliance with each of these laws.

The Rehabilitation Act was passed in 1973 to prohibit employment discrimination based on physical or mental disabilities. This legislation charges employers with taking affirmative action to hire qualified disabled persons. The act further requires that reasonable accommodation(s) be made for the disabled unless the employer can show an undue hardship based on business necessity or financial cost (spending in excess of $1,000 per employee). The Civil Service Commission, Department of Labor, Department of Veterans Affairs, and the Department of Health and Human Services administer this law, which applies to the federal government, federal contractors with contracts over $10,000, and companies who are in receipt of funds in excess of $10,000 by a company that receives federal monies.

Under this law, disability is defined as a physical or mental impairment that substantially limits one or more major life activities. Examples of reasonable accommodations that can be made under the Rehabilitation Act consist of the following:

- A change in job design: eliminating tasks that are not really necessary to perform the job
- Qualifications: getting rid of unnecessary job specs for everyone, such as requiring a medical exam prior to employment (which will allow the disabled to be hired)
- Job accessibility: adding wheelchair ramps, brail in elevators, etc.
- Nondiscriminatory treatment: eliminating hiring decisions based on people's fear of, or uneasiness with, disabilities

Applicant Databases

An **applicant tracking system** is a method used to make the selection process more effective by utilizing a software application to electronically process a company's recruitment needs. An applicant tracking system allows an organization to do this by sorting through large numbers of resumes that are submitted in order to find the candidates who are the best possible fit for a specific open position, based on a search for certain keywords. This allows employers to stay better organized, save time, and stay on top of the hiring process.

All institutions that receive federal contracts are required to track what is known as **applicant flow data**. This is information collected on the gender and race of all applicants who apply for open positions within an organization. The goal of collecting such data is to be able to perform an analysis of differences in selection rates among various groups for a specific position, to ensure a proper demographic pool is being sourced for the role. This data can be collected by the use of an Equal Employment Opportunity (EEO) information form. Employers must make a reasonable effort to obtain this information. It is important to note that any such type of information obtained is not to be used in hiring decisions. It is for Human Resources' eyes only and cannot be kept with an employee's application or personnel file. This is clearly disclosed in the application, so that the applicant is aware that the company is not basing their hiring decision on demographic information the applicant shares.

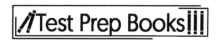

Recruitment Sources and Methods

Recruiting refers to procedures and strategies designed to encourage and find potential, qualified candidates who seek employment. If the labor pool is unsuitable, then reaching these staffing goals is impossible, and so recruiting is essential for any organization's staffing plan.

An organization usually uses three types of recruiting: external, internal, and alternative. **External recruiting** seeks individuals from outside the organization for employment and usually emphasizes the advantages of employment with the organization, advertising benefits such as pay, insurance, leave, or employee discounts. **Internal recruiting** encourages individuals from within the organization to seek transfers or promotions to fill vacant positions. **Alternative recruiting** seeks candidates from internships or temps to perform specific tasks for a limited period of time.

When a company seeks to recruit from within, some of the most common strategies to find potential candidates include internal announcements, which are made to employees before the general public; job bidding, which involves an employee expressing an interested in a position, whether or not it is available; and promotion plans, which detail an employee's skills and training and future positions for which they're qualified.

While the majority of companies will recruit in the ways that are mentioned above, some may look elsewhere to find the required number of candidates. Some of these methods include:

- Passing out fliers
- Recruiting in professional organizations
- Finding employees through prison work programs
- Recruiting outgoing employees from a company's clients, vendors, or suppliers
- Offering sign-on bonuses to prospective employees

The labor pool of available candidates can further be classified into three categories: active, semi-active, and passive.

Active candidates are those engaging in a search for new employment, whether they're already employed or unemployed. Most often these individuals are looking for new opportunities, concerned about their current employer's stability due to their employer's outsourcing, bankruptcy, etc. The most common method employers use to reach active candidates is through job postings. Using social media can aid in reaching the highest audience possible but can sometimes also attract a large number of unqualified candidates. Another recruiting method involves active sourcing, which is made easier as these candidates are looking to be noticed. Again, using social media such as LinkedIn is an effective way in finding these jobseekers.

Semi-active candidates are not actively looking for work but are preparing themselves for new opportunities. These individuals most often do not have a resume prepared, and businesses looking to recruit them often allow submissions of alternatives, such as an online social media profile.

Passive candidates are employed but not looking for work. These individuals are sometimes still worth pursuing by employers, if candidates are willing to listen to a recruiter about a better career opportunity. Proactive searching is the most effective way of reaching this group, again, through avenues like social media.

Employee Referral

Employee referrals can serve as a great tool when recruiting for positions requiring specialized skills that are difficult to fill via regular recruiting methods. Individuals who interview via employee referrals typically know what to expect regarding the work environment from their interactions with the employees who already work there, so there are fewer surprises. Employees who refer candidates usually benefit from a monetary incentive and can experience increased loyalty because they are having a "say" in the building of the workplace culture. It is important for a company not to rely solely on employee referrals to fill all open positions, so as to avoid creating cliques throughout the workplace. Such groups typically include individuals who are very similar to one another, which limits innovation.

Social Networking/Social Media

Social networking/media is a great tool for locating both passive and active candidates. LinkedIn, Facebook, and Twitter are the three most popular social media sites. However, other social media sites, such as Instagram, are quickly gaining more attention. A company's social media recruiting strategy allows candidates to view job openings and gain a better understanding of the company's personality and culture. It is important for companies to designate an individual who will respond to candidates' questions and concerns in a timely manner. In addition, a company's social media efforts can be easily monitored (i.e., page likes, number of followers, etc.) to analyze what is truly working, and then adjust strategy accordingly.

Diversity Groups

Organizations are also working to recruit potential employees via various **diversity groups**, which also help to further promote their inclusion efforts. Examples include groups for African Americans, Asian Americans, Latino Americans, disability awareness, LGBTQIA (lesbian, gay, bisexual, transgender, questioning, intersex, and allies), former members of the military, multicultural, emerging professionals, and women.

Alternative Staffing Practices

Outsourcing

Outsourcing is the practice of delegating work responsibilities in a business to a separate third-party individual or organization not associated with the company.

There are three different types of outsourcing:

- Onshore: The vendor is located within the same country as the business
- Nearshore: The vendor is in a country adjacent to the business
- Offshore: The vendor is in a country far from the business

Frequently, a company will outsource when:

- The expertise needed for a specific task cannot be found within the business
- Cost-cutting is needed
- A greater focus on in-business operations is needed

Outsourcing work does have a disadvantage in that the company may find it difficult to monitor the third-party business's operations as opposed to its own employees. Additionally, there is a risk in entrusting business confidentiality to a third party not near the business at all—especially with elements such as financial information. It is also worth noting that the idea of outsourcing can decrease morale for onsite employees. They may become worried about their own job security, so it's important for employers to introduce the concept carefully.

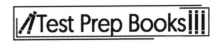

Job Sharing

Job sharing involves two or more employees performing the tasks of a role normally performed by one person. Usually the individuals are employed on a part-time basis. Job sharing has become more prevalent in recent times due to an evolving work culture and the development of alternative work arrangements.

Candidates looking for a work/life balance may see benefits in job sharing, even though the pay is lower and benefits are fewer. Consequently, overall productivity can increase for the business. However, it is essential for the individuals involved to have excellent communication with each other in order to succeed in a role normally designated for one person.

Phased Retirement

Phased retirement for older employees involves both the cutting back of working hours (or days of work) and the phasing in of retirement benefits such as Social Security funds. Phased retirement arrangements can take the form of part-time work, temporary or seasonal work, or job sharing.

Most commonly, these are informal agreements between an employer and an employee. A possible reason for the lack of formalized programs is the lack of legislation regarding regulations of benefits and salary coverage for potential retirees.

Phased retirement benefits employers by allowing more senior employees with years of workplace knowledge and experience to train their replacements over time.

Interviewing Techniques

Behavioral Interviews

The **behavioral interview** technique involves interviewers asking candidates to use specific examples to describe how they have handled a problem or performed a task in a past work situation. The thought behind this method is that past behavior is the best predictor of future job performance. Examples of behavioral-based interview questions are: "Can you tell me about a time when you had to go above and beyond the call of duty to get a job done?" and "Tell me about the last time you tackled a project that demanded a lot of initiative." Candidates can best answer these types of questions by using the STAR method, meaning they describe the past Situation or Task, explain the Action(s) they took, and describe the Results they achieved. It has been found that responses to questions about candidates' actual, past experiences tend to have high validity.

Situational Interviews

Situational interviews relate more to hypothetical situations that may take place in the future. For example, an employer may present a problem that could occur in the position for which the candidate is interviewing and ask the applicant how they might handle it. While this type of interview is useful in determining the candidate's suitability for the position, situational interviews can neglect an applicant's past work experience.

Panel Interviews

Panel interviews are conducted by a group of individuals from the organization that may consist of managers, Human Resources representatives, and other future team members, in order to better evaluate whether or not a candidate is suitable. Panel interviews can help to reduce personal biases in the selection decision and are especially useful in work environments where teamwork is an important factor. This type of interview also gives candidates the opportunity to meet more people from the company and see how they interact with each other.

Post-Offer Activities

Once a new employee is hired, a number of activities need to be completed for that individual to have a smooth transition into the organization. Some of the typical post-offer activities include:

- Perform any other necessary background checks
- Make copies of the offer letter
- Work with IT and other internal departments to prepare for the new employee's arrival (establish the workstation, create an email account, etc.)
- Prepare the new hire's packet of paperwork that they will need to complete on the first day
- Work to develop an on-boarding plan that includes a list of important people in the company that the new hire should meet
- Inform any internal applicants who were not selected for the position and provide them with feedback
- Notify any external applicants who were not selected for the role

Executing Employment Agreements

Employment-at-will is always presumed when a written employment agreement does not exist; it is a common-law doctrine that states employers have the right to hire, promote, demote, or fire whomever they choose, provided there is not a law or contract in place to the contrary. Under this doctrine, employees are also free to leave an employer whenever they choose to seek other employment.

There are two types of employment contracts (agreements): implied and express. **Implied contracts** are inferred from an employer's conduct or actions. An example of an implied contract is when an employer promises an employee job security or hires an employee for an indefinite timeframe. An employee expectation is established, especially when the employer and the employee have enjoyed a long-term business relationship.

An **express contract** is based on an employer's written or oral words and is a formal agreement that outlines the details of the employment arrangement. In the past, these types of contracts were reserved for executive and senior management positions. Now they are also being used for technical and highly specialized employees who possess skills that are harder to come by.

Completing I-9/E-Verify Process

Companies must be vigilant in their verification of new hires' right to work in the United States and their identities via the I-9 process within the first three days of employment. Because timeliness is of the essence, the Department of Homeland Security runs a government program to assist with this process; it is called E-Verify. At the current time, use of E-Verify is only mandatory for government contractors and subcontractors. For more information about I-9, please see the content under *Immigration Reform and Control Act (IRCA)* content of the *Federal Laws and Regulations* portion of this section.

Coordinate Relocations

Many companies offer relocation benefits to assist new hires during a very stressful time in their lives. Such benefits can include any or all of the following:

- Paying for temporary living expenses
- Reimbursing for moving fees
- Assisting a "trailing spouse" with their job search
- Allowing for the use of a company car
- Providing financial assistance with selling a home (or buying a new home)

Immigration

Organizations are held responsible for the verification of their new hires' credentials and identities. They must ensure that the documents presented to them (i.e., visas, passports, Social Security cards, etc.) are indeed official and are not fabricated in any way. At any time, the U.S. Immigration and Customs Enforcement (ICE) can audit a company's records to guarantee compliance with employment eligibility laws. If a company's Human Resources department is found with fraudulent documents, the company can be held liable. For more information about immigration, please see the *Immigration Reform and Control Act (IRCA)* content of the *Federal Laws and Regulations* portion of this section.

Orientation and On-Boarding

Orientation

Orientation is part of the administrative, transactional aspect of the overall on-boarding process, focused on having employees complete the following types of tasks within their first couple of days of employment:

- Have their photograph taken to create their corporate ID badge
- Take a tour of the building in which they will be working on a daily basis
- Complete I-9 verification
- Register for health care and other company benefits
- Participate in training on the company's time entry system
- Gain an understanding of the payroll process
- Review the company's history, vision, and mission, along with key policies and procedures
- Receive and sign off on a copy of their formal job description

It is also important to note that the workspace for new hires is often set up in advance with the necessary office supplies and a welcome note or card to ensure as smooth of a transition as possible.

On-Boarding

On-boarding, also known as **organizational socialization**, is the process by which new hires obtain the knowledge, skills, and behaviors they need in order to become valued, productive contributors to the company. The success of on-boarding programs is crucial because new employees decide whether or not to stay with an organization during their first six months of work. Therefore, it is important for companies to make an effort to ensure that new employees feel supported and get adjusted to the social and performance aspects of their new roles quickly.

On-boarding can begin by having an employee's new managers and teammates reach out to them via email to welcome them even prior to their formal start date with the company. On the first day at work, the manager can introduce the new hire to the team member who will serve as their "buddy," to whom they can feel free to go to with any questions or concerns. Taking the new hire out of the office for a welcome lunch on the first day with a couple of staff members is always a nice gesture, as well as ensuring they have lunch partners for the first couple of weeks on the job.

Other aspects of successful on-boarding programs involve the new hire's manager scheduling meet-and-greet appointments to learn more about the roles that each teammate in the department plays and how the new hire will interact with them. These types of meetings can also be scheduled with individuals throughout the company who have key relationships with the department, such as members of IT, Marketing, Human Resources, etc. Additionally, providing the new hire with an on-boarding schedule that involves various team members who will train on various processes and applications can be helpful. It is also important for the manager to meet with the new hire to discuss their performance and development plans for the first three months, to provide clear expectations. Finally, to help a new hire build contacts throughout the company, it is imperative to get them involved in a cross-functional project.

There is no set time limit for on-boarding programs, but at some companies, these programs can last throughout an employee's first year.

Practice Questions

1. Which of the following activities is an example of downsizing?
   a. Implementing a hiring freeze.
   b. Reducing the number of hierarchical levels.
   c. Utilizing contingent workers to fill in.
   d. Outsourcing work to an external service provider.

2. A detailed description of specific qualifications, experience, or education that is needed to perform tasks is known as which of the following?
   a. Job description
   b. Job specification
   c. Job competency
   d. Job analysis

3. A detailed list of broad skills or traits needed for a position is known as which of the following?
   a. Job analysis
   b. Job description
   c. Job competency
   d. Job specification

4. Tasks and responsibilities that are fundamental to a specific position are known as which of the following?
   a. Job competencies
   b. Marginal job functions
   c. Job specifications
   d. Essential job functions

5. Which type of interview occurs when an interviewer has guided conversations with applicants that involve broad questions and new questions that come about from the discussions that take place?
   a. Semi-structured
   b. Structured
   c. Non-directive
   d. Unstructured

6. Which type of interview utilizes questions that are developed from an applicant's answers to previous questions?
   a. Unstructured
   b. Nondirective
   c. Semi-structured
   d. Structured

7. Which of the following pre-employment activities can assist companies with protecting themselves from lawsuits or damage to their reputation?
   a. Interviewing
   b. Selection tests
   c. Reference and background checks
   d. Employment agreements

8. Which of the following items is inferred from an employer's actions or conduct?
   a. Express contract
   b. Employment-at-will
   c. Golden parachute clause
   d. Implied contract

9. Which of the following employers is required to have an affirmative action plan in place?
   a. An employer who has sixty employees and $55,000 in federal contracts
   b. An employer with $40,000 in federal contracts
   c. An employer with fifty-five employees
   d. An employer who is part of the Department of Transportation

10. Which of the following is the major element of an affirmative action plan that examines the internal and external population of women and minorities to determine their theoretical opportunity for employment?
   a. Utilization analysis
   b. Availability analysis
   c. Job group analysis
   d. Organizational profile

11. Which of the following is the major element of an affirmative action plan that compares the availability of women and minorities to their current representation within each job group at the company?
   a. Availability analysis
   b. Job group analysis
   c. Utilization analysis
   d. Organizational profile

12. Under federal guidelines, under what length of time is an employer required to keep employment applications and resumes?
   a. Three years
   b. One year
   c. Three years after creation or following the hire/no hire decision (whichever date is later)
   d. One year after creation or following the hire/no hire decision (whichever date is later)

13. Under federal guidelines, under what length of time is an employer required to keep employee records associated with employment benefits?
   a. Six years
   b. Three years
   c. Five years
   d. One year

14. Under federal guidelines, under what length of time is an employer required to keep employee records associated with family medical leave?
   a. One year
   b. Three years
   c. Five years
   d. Two years

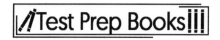

15. Which of the following statements is true regarding Title VII of the Civil Rights Act of 1964?
   a. Equal working conditions must be provided to all employees.
   b. Discrimination against sex and race is prohibited.
   c. All employees must be provided with an equal opportunity to participate in training.
   d. Sexual harassment training must be provided to all employees.

16. Which of the following would MOST likely be considered an essential job function?
   a. An employee participates in an ongoing employee committee assignment as time permits.
   b. An employee devotes approximately 8 percent of her time to making cold calls to obtain new business.
   c. An employee delegates preparation of a template to their administrative support.
   d. An employee regularly reviews engineering design documents.

17. Which of the following situations would more than likely warrant a written employment contract?
   a. An employee who is a salesperson
   b. A full-time telecommuting employee
   c. An employee who is a department manager
   d. An employee who is a graphic artist

18. Before extending a contingent offer of employment, an employer should obtain which of the following?
   a. Medical records and completion of a physical examination
   b. Signed consent from the candidate to check work references
   c. Verbal consent from the candidate to check work references
   d. Polygraph test

19. Which of the following is an exception to Title VII of the Civil Rights Act of 1964?
   a. An employer with only twenty employees
   b. A new seniority system that is being implemented at a workplace
   c. A bona fide occupational qualification
   d. A work-related requirement that is not truly legitimate

Answer Explanations

1. A: Implementing a hiring freeze is an activity that is an example of downsizing. Reducing the number of hierarchical levels, Choice *B*, is an example of corporate restructuring. Utilizing contingent workers to fill in (Choice *C*) and outsourcing work to an external service provider (Choice *D*) are examples of workforce expansion.

2. B: Job specification is a detailed description of specific qualifications, experience, or education that is needed to perform tasks. Choice *A*, job description, is a detailed breakdown of specific tasks, skills, and knowledge required for a position. Job competency, Choice *C*, is a detailed list of broad skills or traits needed for a position. Finally, job analysis, Choice *D*, is a way of gathering and analyzing information systemically about the context, content, and human resource requirements of jobs within an organization.

3. C: Job competency is a detailed list of broad skills or traits needed for a position. Job analysis, Choice *A*, is a way of gathering and analyzing information systemically about the context, content, and human resource requirements of jobs within an organization. Job description, Choice *B*, is a detailed breakdown of specific tasks, skills and knowledge required for a position. Finally, job specification, Choice *D*, is a detailed description of specific qualifications, experience, or education that is needed to perform tasks.

4. D: Essential job functions are tasks and responsibilities that are fundamental to a specific position. Job competencies, Choice *A*, are detailed lists of broad skills or traits needed for positions. Marginal job functions, Choice *B*, are duties that are ancillary or incidental to the nature or purpose of a job. Finally, job specifications, Choice *C*, are detailed descriptions of specific qualifications, experience, or education that is needed to perform tasks.

5. A: A semi-structured interview occurs when an interviewer has guided conversations with applicants that involve broad questions and new questions that come about from the discussions that take place. A structured interview, Choice *B*, is controlled by the interviewer, who has a list of specific, job-related questions prepared prior to the start of the interview. The same questions are asked of all applicants. A non-directive interview, Choice *C*, utilizes questions that are developed from an applicant's answers to previous questions. Finally, Choice *D*, an unstructured interview, takes place when an interviewer improvises and asks applicants questions that were not prepared prior to the start of the interview.

6. B: A non-directive interview utilizes questions that are developed from an applicant's answers to previous questions. An unstructured interview, Choice *A*, takes place when an interviewer improvises and asks applicants questions that were not prepared prior to the start of the interview. A semi-structured interview, Choice *C*, occurs when an interviewer has guided conversations with applicants that involve broad questions and new questions that come about from the discussions that take place. Finally, a structured interview, Choice *D*, is controlled by the interviewer, who has a list of specific, job-related questions prepared prior to the start of the interview. The same questions are asked of all applicants.

7. C: Reference and background checks are pre-employment activities that can assist companies with protecting themselves from lawsuits or damage to their reputation (for example, in the event of negligent hiring claims). Interviewing candidates, Choice *A*, may not reveal all pertinent information. Choices *B* and *D*, selection tests and employment agreements, do not provide information that would protect the company's interests.

8. D: An implied contract is inferred from an employer's actions or conduct. An express contract, Choice *A*, is based on an employer's written or oral words. Employment-at-will, Choice *B*, is a common-law doctrine that states employers have the right to hire, promote, demote, or fire whomever they choose, provided there is not a law or contract in place to the contrary. Under this doctrine, employees are also free to leave an employer whenever they choose to seek other employment. Finally, a golden parachute clause, Choice *C*, is an agreement between an employer and an executive that guarantees the executive the right to certain benefits if their employment is terminated.

9. A: Employers with fifty or more employees and $50,000 in federal contracts are required to have affirmative action plans in place, as well as employers who are a member of the federal banking system and employers who issue, sell, or redeem U.S. Savings Bonds.

10. B: An availability analysis is the major element of an affirmative action plan that examines the internal and external population of women and minorities to determine their theoretical opportunity for employment. A utilization analysis, Choice *A*, compares the availability of women and minorities to their current representation within each job group at the company. A job group analysis, Choice *C*, is a list of all titles that comprise each job group. Jobs are grouped according to whether they have similar content, responsibilities, compensation, and opportunities for advancement. Choice *D*, an organizational profile, is a snapshot of an organization and organizes the key components and competitions within that organization.

11. C: A utilization analysis is the major element of an affirmative action plan that compares the availability of women and minorities to their current representation within each job group at the company. An availability analysis, Choice *A*, examines the internal and external population of women and minorities to determine their theoretical opportunity for employment. A job group analysis, Choice *B*, is a list of all titles that comprise each job group. Jobs are grouped according to whether they have similar content, responsibilities, wage rates, and opportunities for advancement. Finally, an organizational profile, Choice *D*, depicts the organization's staffing patterns to determine if any barriers exist to equal opportunity employment.

12. D: Under federal guidelines, an employer is required to keep employment applications and resumes for one year after creation or following the hire/no hire decision (whichever date is later).

13. A: Under federal guidelines, an employer is required to keep records associated with employment benefits for a period of six years.

14. B: Under federal guidelines, an employer is required to keep records associated with family medical leave for a period of three years.

15. B: Title VII of the Civil Rights Act of 1964 prohibits discrimination against sex and race.

16. D: When an employee regularly reviews engineering design documents, this would most likely be considered an essential job function.

17. A: An employee who is a salesperson would more than likely warrant a written employment contract to outline information, such as salary (including guaranteed or discretionary bonuses), commission structure and payment processes, and clauses referencing non-compete agreements.

18. B: An employer should obtain signed consent from the candidate to check work references before extending a contingent offer of employment. This is due to the fact that many companies have been sued by job applicants who have discovered that they have been given poor references. Physical examinations cannot be required by an employer until after a job offer has been made. Finally, polygraph tests cannot be required by the majority of employers.

19. C: A bona fide occupational qualification is an exception to Title VII of the Civil Rights Act of 1964. This act applies to most employers with fifteen or more employees. A new seniority system implemented in the workplace and work-related requirements that are not truly legitimate are not exceptions to Title VII of the Civil Rights Act of 1964.

Compensation and Benefits

Rules and Regulations Related to Compensation and Benefits

Payroll Vendors

Some of the reasons that companies may elect to outsource their payroll function include the following:

- Freeing up staff time to allow resources to be more strategic in nature
- To reduce costs
- To improve compliance
- Possibly to avoid fines associated with incorrect/late payments or IRS filings
- To have the ability to offer direct deposit of payroll checks to employees

An employer can choose to outsource its entire payroll function or only one or more areas of its payroll function, such as W-2 form printing services. When outsourcing payroll, an employer should select a vendor with an excellent reputation for paying employees on time and providing a high level of customer service.

In an effort not to create additional work, it is important to determine if the vendor's systems are able to effectively integrate with the employer's systems—e.g., time tracking and self-service technologies used to update employees' personal data and payroll-related information. An employer should ensure that the vendor chosen will be able to provide the level of service that the company requires at an affordable cost.

COBRA Administration

When administering COBRA, the length of time that an employee is eligible for coverage is determined by the type of qualifying event. For example, eighteen months is the period of eligibility for an employee's reduction in hours or an employee's termination, while twenty-nine months is the period of eligibility for the disablement of an employee. Additionally, thirty-six months is the period of eligibility for a divorce/legal separation or death of an employed spouse, as well as for a dependent child who loses eligibility status under the plan rules. Employees and their family members have sixty days to elect COBRA coverage from the time that a qualifying event has taken place.

Covered employers are required to provide an initial COBRA notice within ninety days of the date an employee/spouse is covered under the plan. Employers are also required to provide a notice of unavailability of continuation of coverage within fourteen days of the date of the qualifying event, if the employee/spouse is not covered. Employees must be notified of their coverage ending before the maximum continuous period allowed.

Employee Recognition Vendors

Due to a lack of staff resources, time, or in-house expertise, companies may choose to outsource their employee rewards program to a trusted recognition vendor. Since a vendor can, ultimately, determine the success or failure of a company's rewards program, there are a number of items that an employer should evaluate when entering into this type of relationship.

An exceptional recognition vendor will take the time to learn about a company's culture, business goals, employee rewards needs, and program budget. The recognition vendor should have an offering of high-quality awards and be able to accommodate rush orders and unique awards, if needed.

Additionally, world-class customer service is the key to employees receiving timely reward fulfillment and recognition for their efforts and achievements. An employer should be assured that the company will receive correct invoices and accurate reporting from the vendor. The ultimate goal for both the employer and the recognition vendor is to ensure that employees feel valued and remain loyal.

Non-Cash Rewards

Managers are frequently being asked to do more with less, including stretching their compensation budgets. This is where non-cash rewards can be factored in with cash compensation to motivate the workforce effectively. Non-cash rewards include such items as personalized thank-you notes for a job well done, company merchandise, and gift cards. Some organizations have factored non-cash rewards into their formal recognition programs, making them more meaningful.

For example, there are peer-to-peer recognition programs in place, where one employee can send a personalized thank-you eCard to another employee for a job well done. In that same system, managers can acknowledge an employee for his or her extra effort on a project by assigning a number of recognition points, along with sending an eCard. Once an employee accumulates a bank of recognition points, they can cash in the points to receive either a gift card or an item from the company store.

Pay Structures and Programs

Differential and Performance-Based Pay (Merit Pay)

Even though it is not required by law under the Fair Labor Standards Act (FLSA), many employers elect to reward their employees in certain situations with compensation that is in addition to their base pay. Pay practices regarding these types of situations vary greatly among employers.

Differential pay programs are used to reward employees for performing work that is viewed as less than desirable. There are time-based and geographic differential pay programs.

- **Time-based differential pay** is allotted to employees based on when they work. For example, some employees receive additional pay, called **shift pay**, for working second or third shift or for being called in to work during an emergency, also known as **emergency shift pay**.
- **Premium pay** is sometimes paid to employees as a higher rate of overtime pay for working holidays or vacation days.
- Employees who work in a risky environment can be paid **hazard pay**.
- **Reporting pay** can be paid to employees who arrive at their place of employment and find that there is no available work for them to perform.
- **Geographic differential pay** is allotted to employees based on where they work. For example, sometimes employers have different pay structures for different locations and pay extra to attract workers to certain locales, such as remote, offshore oil rigs, and institute pay differentials for work in foreign countries.

Performance-based pay plans are used to motivate employees to perform their work at a higher level. Performance-based pay plans can be instituted at the individual, group, and organization-wide levels.

- Examples of **individual performance-based pay plans** are piece rates, commissions, and cash bonuses. These promote productivity (by 30 percent) but do not promote teamwork and may be difficult to measure.
- In **group performance-based pay plans**, an entire group is rewarded for exceeding performance standards and each person in the group receives the same amount of incentive as a percentage of their pay. An example of a group performance-based pay plan is a gainsharing plan, where a portion of the gains an organization realizes from group effort is shared with the group. These promote teamwork but have a moderate impact on productivity (13 percent).
- **Organization-wide performance-based pay plans** are profit-sharing plans, performance-sharing plans, and stock ownership plans. These increase shareholder returns and company profits but generate only a 6 percent increase in productivity.

Non-Cash Compensation

Non-monetary compensation is the category of employee benefits that do not carry tangible value. This includes flexible working schedules, company parties, a nice office, rewarding work, and a supportive work environment.

Pay Structure

Following the completion of job evaluations and the collection of data from salary surveys, a company works to establish an overall pay structure. A **pay structure** provides the overall framework for an organization to use to deliver its total rewards strategy. When creating a pay structure, companies establish pay grades by grouping jobs together that are found to have the same relative internal worth. Jobs within the same pay grade will pay the same rate or within the same pay range. When employers are setting pay ranges, they determine the minimum, midpoint, and maximum compensation for a pay grade and set some overlap between pay ranges.

Not every employee fits perfectly within the set pay ranges. For example, an employee who is paid a **red-circle rate** is paid at a rate above the range maximum. If this tends to be a common occurrence, it may mean that the organization's pay ranges lag the market and need to be re-examined. In contrast, an employee who is paid a **green-circle rate** is paid at a rate below the range minimum.

Total Rewards Statements

Total Rewards plans include things like monetary compensation (salary, bonus, etc.) employee benefits (healthcare, vacation time, retirement, etc.), and personal growth (on- or off-the-job training, career development, etc.). Total rewards plans demand constant reevaluation to ensure that they are providing the most appropriate plan to employees—one that is in line with the organization's philosophy and comparable to those of competitor organizations. One way HR professionals can keep their total rewards plans current and competitive is by referencing total remuneration surveys, which provide market data on compensation and benefits plans from other organizations. HR professionals can use this data for benchmarking purposes when evaluating their own organization's total rewards plans, making adjustments as necessary. In addition to consulting remuneration surveys, HR professionals also need to consider the EVP, which refers to how employees perceive the value of the organization's total rewards plan and other intangible benefits from working for the organization. EVP can be assessed by conducting internal employee surveys. HR can also conduct stay interviews, or interviews with employees to determine which factors drive retention and how they can be improved. If employees know that their input is considered in the design of their total rewards plan, they may be more likely to support the project.

Total Reward Statement

In addition to more formal, organization-wide communications that may take place only a few times a year, ongoing, informal communications should be encouraged between managers and employees. In an effort to make these communications more personal, companies are distributing total reward statements to their employees to demonstrate that their pay is just one piece of the picture.

A **total reward statement** breaks down the rest of an employee's comprehensive benefits package to show them everything that goes into their total compensation, along with the company's contributions towards each of the items. The goal is to show employees an overall picture of the value and associated cost of their total compensation package.

Labor Market Trends

The supply pool from which employers attract new hires is called the **labor market**. Employers must identify the labor markets (i.e., geographic, global, industry-specific, educational, and technical) from which they can recruit candidates based on the jobs that need to be filled, especially for key positions.

An analysis of labor markets during workforce planning has a number of benefits, including:

- Gaining an understanding of the unemployment rate
- Identifying where employers are competing for labor
- Researching salaries paid for certain positions
- Identifying employment trends in a particular industry

The main federal institution that measures and collates nationwide employment data is the Bureau of Labor Statistics within the US Department of Labor. This department has separate state departments that also report state-specific data. Among the data collected are market activity, average salaries, basic job duties, and working conditions.

Implementing Pay, Benefit, Incentive, Separation, and Severance Systems and Programs

Because total rewards plans represent a significant expense to any organization, they can be viewed from a return on investment (ROI) perspective—focusing on how to maximize the returns (employee satisfaction, retention, and value) from the investment (i.e., the rewards). HR professionals must ensure that plans are designed appropriately to meet the needs of employees by first assessing which benefits programs employees place the most value on as well as which benefits align with the organization's philosophy and business strategy. For example, in a sales division, annual bonuses might be aligned with employees' sales performances. Before implementing any performance-based rewards, though, the performance measures that will be appraised must first be clearly defined. In an organization that values internal advancement, an important benefit might be free employee training and educational opportunities. In designing and implementing monetary compensation rewards in particular, HR begins with a clear description of a job (its responsibilities, knowledge, and skills) and then determines the internal and external value of that position. Salary, raises, bonuses, separation, and severance pay should all be considered when designing a monetary compensation system.

Federal Laws and Regulations

A company's total rewards strategy is used to attract, motivate, engage, and retain employees through compensation packages made up of pay, incentives, and benefits. This rewards system should be aligned with the company's mission, strategy, and corporate culture, and it must comply with all applicable laws and regulations.

Davis Bacon Act (1931)

This piece of legislation applies to contractors and subcontractors working on federally funded contracts in excess of $2,000. The act requires employers to pay all laborers at construction sites—associated with such contracts—at least the prevailing wage and fringe benefits that individuals working in similar projects in the area are receiving. Employers who fail to comply with this act risk losing their federal contracts and the ability to receive new federal contracts for a period of up to three years.

Walsh-Healey Public Contracts Act (1936)

This federal law applies to contractors working on federally funded supply contracts in excess of $10,000. Under this act, employers associated with such contracts must pay employees at least the federal **minimum wage**—currently set at $7.25 per hour—and overtime pay. Overtime pay is calculated as one and one-half times an individual's regular rate of pay for any hours worked in excess of eight hours in a single workday or any hours worked in excess of forty hours in a single workweek.

The employment of youth under the age of sixteen and convicts is also prohibited under this legislation. Additionally, the act calls for job safety and sanitation protocols. Failure to comply with this law may result in the withholding of contract payments to reimburse any underpayment of wages or overtime pay due to employees. There is also a penalty of $10 per person per day for any employer who is found to be employing youth or convicts, along with possible additional legal action. Employers may ultimately face losing their federal contracts and the ability to receive new federal contracts for a period of up to three years for non-compliance.

Fair Labor Standards Act (1938)

The **Fair Labor Standards Act** (**FLSA**) is also known as the **Wage and Hour Law**, and it covers most governmental agencies and private-sector employers. This includes companies with employees involved in interstate commerce, employers with $500,000 or more in annual sales or business completed, and organizations caring for the physically and mentally ill, the aging population, and educational institutions. The act does not apply to employers working in industries who are covered under other labor standards that are specific to those industries. The law was put into effect to establish employee classification and to regulate minimum wage, overtime pay, on-call pay, associated recordkeeping, and child labor, as discussed in detail below.

Minimum Wage

Under this act, employers must pay nonexempt employees at least the federal minimum wage. However, if the state in which an employee works pays a higher minimum wage than the current federal minimum wage, the employee will receive the higher state minimum wage. Additionally, employers must pay $2.13 per hour in direct wages to employees who receive tips as their form of salary. The total of the employer's wage and the employee's tips should then equal the minimum wage.

Overtime

Under this law, employers must pay nonexempt employees overtime pay at the rate of one and one-half times an individual's regular rate of pay for any hours worked in excess of forty hours of work in a single workweek. The act does not require that overtime be paid to employees for work performed on Saturdays, Sundays, or paid time-off days, such as sick days, vacation days, or holidays. Overtime pay that is earned in a specific workweek must be paid out in the pay period during which it was earned, instead of averaging overtime hours across multiple workweeks.

On-Call

Under this act, employers must pay nonexempt employees their regular rate of pay for **on-call time**—the time that they are required to remain at the employer's place of business while waiting to engage in work as required by their employer. An example of this would be medical employees who are asked by their employer to wait to engage in work in an on-call room at a hospital. Since they are not free to leave the hospital and are expected to work if called upon, they must be compensated for their time spent on-call.

Record Keeping

Under this law, employers are required to keep specific records as defined by the Department of Labor. In regard to nonexempt employees, employers must specifically keep track of the following personal information for an employee:

- Name, address, occupation, gender, and date of birth, if employee is under the age of nineteen
- Day and time of the start of the workweek
- Total hours an employee worked during each workday and for the workweek as a whole
- Employee's daily and weekly straight-time earnings
- Employee's regular hourly rate of pay for weeks when any overtime is worked
- Total overtime pay for the workweek
- Any additions or deductions to an employee's wages
- Total wages paid to an employee during each pay period
- Date the employee received payment for work performed and the pay period that payment covered

Child Labor

This legislation also put provisions in place—commonly referred to as **child labor laws**—to ensure that working youth were guaranteed a safe workplace environment that did not pose a risk to their overall health and wellbeing or prevent them from pursuing additional educational opportunities.

Youth under the age of fourteen are only allowed to perform such functions as newspaper delivery, babysitting, acting, and assisting in their parents' business, as long as that business is non-hazardous in nature. They may also perform non-hazardous agricultural work on a farm that employs one of their parents. Youth ages fourteen and fifteen are allowed to perform non-hazardous work, such as positions in retail, some yard work, and some kitchen and food service work. Youth in this age group are not allowed to work more than three hours a day or eighteen hours a week when school is in session. However, when school is not in session, these youth can work up to eight hours a day and up to forty hours a week.

Youth in this age group do have restricted work hours of 7:00 am to 7:00 pm during the school year. The evening time is extended to 9:00 pm during the period of June 1 through Labor Day. Youth ages sixteen and seventeen can work unlimited hours. However, youth in this age group are still prohibited from working on hazardous jobs, such as operating trash binders, shredders, or material-handling equipment.

<table>
<tr><th>Age</th><th>Legal Requirements</th></tr>
<tr><td>Under 14</td><td><ul><li>Children under fourteen years of age may not be employed in non-agricultural occupations covered by the FLSA, including food service establishments. Permissible employment for such children is limited to work that is exempt from the FLSA (such as delivering newspapers to the consumer and acting). Children may also perform work not covered by the FLSA such as completing minor chores around private homes or casual babysitting.</li></ul></td></tr>
<tr><td>14 & 15</td><td><ul><li>14 and 15-year-olds may be employed in restaurants and quick-service establishments outside school hours in a variety of jobs for limited periods of time and under specified conditions. Child Labor Regulations No. 3, 29 C.F.R. 570, Subpart C, limits both the time of day and number of hours this age group may be employed as well as the types of jobs they may perform.</li><li>Hours and times of day standards for the employment of 14- and 15-year-olds:</li><li>outside school hours; school hours are determined by the local public school in the area the minor is residing while employed;</li><li>no more than three hours on a school day, including Fridays;</li><li>no more than eight hours on a non-school day;</li><li>no more than eighteen hours during a week when school is in session;</li><li>no more than forty hours during a week when school is not in session;</li><li>between 7 a.m. and 7 p.m., except between June 1 and Labor Day when the evening hour is extended to 9 p.m.</li></ul>Occupation standards for the employment of 14- and 15-year-olds:<ul><li>They may perform cashiering, shelf stocking, and the bagging and carrying out of customer orders.</li><li>They may perform clean-up work, including the use of vacuum cleaners and floor waxers.</li><li>They may perform limited cooking duties involving electric or gas grills that do not entail cooking over an open flame. They may also cook with deep fat fryers that are equipped with and utilize devices that automatically raise and lower the “baskets” into and out of the hot grease of oil. They may not operate</li></ul></td></tr>
</table>

<table>
<tr><th>Age</th><th>Legal Requirements</th></tr>
<tr><td></td><td>NEXCO broilers, rotisseries, pressure cookers, fryolaters, high-speed ovens, or rapid toasters.
• They may not perform any baking activities.
• They may not work in warehousing or load or unload goods to or from trucks or conveyors.
• They may not operate, clean, set up, adjust, repair, or oil power driven machines including food slicers, grinders, processors, or mixers.
• They may clean kitchen surfaces and non-power-driven equipment, and filter, transport, and dispose of cooking oil, but only when the temperature of the surface and oils do not exceed 100 degrees Fahrenheit.
• They may not operate power-driven lawn mowers or cutters, or load or unload goods to or from trucks or conveyors.
• They may not work in freezers or meat coolers, but they may occasionally enter a freezer momentarily to retrieve items.
• They are prohibited from working in any of the Hazardous Orders.</td></tr>
<tr><td>16 & 17</td><td>• 16 and 17-year-olds may be employed for unlimited hours in any occupation other than those declared hazardous by the Secretary of Labor. Examples of equipment declared hazardous in food service establishments include:
• Power-Driven Meat and Poultry Processing Machines (meat slicers, meat saws, patty forming machines, meat grinders, and meat choppers): commercial mixers and certain power-driven bakery machines. Employees under eighteen years of age are not permitted to operate, feed, set up, adjust, repair, or clean any of these machines or their disassembled parts.
• Balers and Compactors: Minors under eighteen years of age may not load, operate, or unload balers or compactors. 16 and 17-year-olds may load, but not operate or unload, certain scrap paper balers and paper box compactors under certain specific circumstances.
• Motor Vehicles: Generally, no employee under 18 years of age may drive on the job or serve as an outside helper on a motor vehicle on a public road, but seventeen-year-olds who meet certain specific requirements may drive automobiles and trucks that do not exceed 6,000 pounds gross vehicle weight for limited amounts of time as part of their job. Such minors are, however, prohibited from making time sensitive deliveries (such as pizza deliveries or other trips where time is of the essence) and from driving at night.</td></tr>
<tr><td>18</td><td>• Once a youth reaches 18 years of age, he or she is no longer subject to the federal child labor provisions.</td></tr>
</table>

Employers who fail to comply with the FLSA may face lawsuits from both the Secretary of Labor and wronged employees for the repayment of backpay of proper minimum wages and/or overtime pay. If it is found that an employer willfully violated this law, the Department of Labor can also impose an $1,100 penalty per violation for repeated offenses.

Portal-to-Portal Act (1947)

This amendment to the Fair Labor Standards Act (FLSA) deals with the **preliminary tasks**—activities prior to the start of principal workday activities—and **postliminary tasks**—activities following the completion of principal workday activities.

- Examples of postliminary tasks include on-call or standby time, meals and breaks, travel time, and training time. The act requires employers to pay employees who are covered under the Fair Labor Standards Act for time spent traveling to perform job-related tasks, if that travel is outside of the employees' regular work commute.
- Employers must also pay employees for any time they spend waiting to start work when requested to do so by their employer. Additionally, employees are to be paid for hours spent in job-related training that is outside of their normal workday.

Employers who fail to comply with this law may face consequences similar to those detailed above in the FLSA section.

Equal Pay Act (1963)

This law requires employers to pay equal wages to both men and women who perform equal jobs in the same establishment. The job titles need not be identical, but rather, the content of the jobs that must be equal in nature. Equivalent jobs are required to have equal skill, working conditions, effort, and responsibility defined as follows:

- Skill: The educational and professional background of the employee performing the job, combined with his or her ability and training
- Working conditions: The physical surroundings in which the work is performed, along with any associated hazards
- Effort: A measurement of the physical or mental exertion that an employee needs to have in order to perform his or her job
- Responsibility: The employee's degree of accountability in performing his or her job

The act does allow for pay differentials when based on other factors other than gender, such as seniority, merit, production quantities or quality, and geographic work differentials. If brought into question, the employer is faced with the burden to prove that these types of **affirmative defenses** do indeed apply.

If there is a need to correct a difference in pay, an employee cannot be penalized by having his or her pay reduced. Rather, the lower-paid employee's pay rate must be increased. Employers who fail to comply with this act may face up to $10,000 in fines and/or imprisonment up to six months.

Older Workers Benefit Protection Act (1990)

The **Older Workers Benefit Protection Act** (**OWBPA**) was passed as an amendment to the Age Discrimination in Employment Act (ADEA) of 1967. Under this act, it is illegal for employers to discriminate based on an employee's age in the provision of benefits, such as pension programs, retirement plans, or life insurance. The goal is for companies to offer equal benefits to all employees, regardless of age. However, when it can be justified by substantial cost considerations, an employer can reduce benefits to older workers.

The OWBPA also prevents older workers from waiving rights when it comes to the topic of severance agreements. An older worker is to be given twenty-one days for the purpose of consulting with an attorney and considering a severance agreement, which turns into forty-five days for group terminations. An older worker then has seven days after signing such an agreement in which they can revoke the agreement if they change their mind.

The releases associated with these agreements must reference ADEA age discrimination claims. This limits an employer's lawsuit exposure should an employee decide to challenge the criteria that was used to make decisions about which employees were retained and which employees were let go. Employers who fail to comply with this act may face both civil and criminal penalties.

Retirement Equity Act (1984)

This amendment to the Employee Retirement Income Security Act (ERISA) was passed to address concerns around the needs of divorced spouses, surviving spouses, and employees who left the workforce for some period of time to raise a family. Automatic survivor benefits were now required of qualified pension plans in the event of a plan participant's death, and the waiver of these benefits could only occur with the consent of both the plan participant and the participant's spouse.

Additionally, pension plans are now required to make benefit payments in accordance with a domestic relations court order to the former spouse of a plan participant. Under this act, plans were no longer allowed to consider maternity or paternity leave as a break in service for the purposes of plan participation or vesting. Employers who fail to comply with this act may face both civil and criminal penalties.

Consolidated Omnibus Budget Reconciliation Act (1986)

The Consolidated Omnibus Budget Reconciliation Act (COBRA) is an amendment to (ERISA) that allows for the continuation of healthcare coverage in the event that such coverage would end due to certain situations, such as the termination of employment, a divorce, or the death of an employee. The act covers employers with twenty or more employees.

Under this law, employees can pay to continue group medical insurance coverage for a period of up to eighteen to thirty-six months, if they elect to do so in a timely manner and pay the full costs of coverage. They can also be charged a 2 percent administrative fee. Employers who fail to comply with this act may face both civil and criminal penalties.

Health Insurance Portability and Accountability Act (1996)

The Health Insurance Portability and Accountability Act (HIPAA) is an amendment (ERISA). It was passed to improve the continuity and portability of healthcare coverage. This act addresses pre-existing medical conditions or those for which an employee or a member of their immediate family received medical advice or treatment during the six-month period prior to their enrollment date into the employer's healthcare plan, such as a serious illness, injury, or pregnancy.

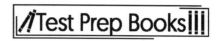

If an employee had creditable healthcare coverage—a group health plan, Medicare, or a military-sponsored healthcare plan—for a period of twelve months, with no lapse in coverage of sixty-three days or more, then an employer cannot refuse them coverage in a new group health plan due to a pre-existing medical condition and cannot charge them a higher rate for coverage. However, if an employee did not previously have creditable healthcare coverage, then an employer can exclude coverage for the treatment of a preexisting medical condition for a period of twelve months—with the exception of pregnancy—or for a period of up to eighteen months for late enrollees in the plan.

Additionally, this act only permits covered entities to use or disclose protected health information for treatment, payment, and healthcare operations. If protected health information is to be released for any other reason, written authorization is required from the patient.

Medical records related to the request for work-related accommodations under the Americans with Disabilities Act (ADA) and leaves of absences under the Family Medical Leave Act (FMLA) are not covered under this law. Employers must have a designated privacy officer who will oversee the organization's privacy policy, along with conducting all necessary training for employees. Employers who fail to comply with this act may face both civil and criminal penalties. Some criminal penalties can cost companies as much as $250,000 and up to ten years in prison.

Patient Protection and Affordable Care Act (2010)

This act—also known as Obamacare, after President Barack Obama—was phased in over a four-year period, making access to healthcare available to several million more Americans. If individuals do not have access to employer-sponsored healthcare coverage, Medicare, or Medicaid, they are now able to purchase healthcare from an insurance exchange and possibly receive a subsidy.

One of the goals of this act is to keep the overall cost of healthcare coverage down by having individuals take advantage of preventative care, such as blood pressure and cholesterol screenings, well-woman visits, and vision screening for all children. Additionally, under this act, children are now permitted to stay under the coverage of their parents' healthcare until the age of twenty-six, and individuals with preexisting medical conditions cannot be denied coverage.

Every American citizen is now required to have health insurance each year or face paying an income tax surcharge. An employer mandate is also being enforced, which is a requirement that all companies employing fifty or more full-time employees provide at least 95 percent of those employees and their dependents with affordable health insurance or be subject to a per-employee fee, based on several factors.

Mental Health Parity Act (1996)

The **Mental Health Parity Act** (**MHPA**) was put into place to ensure that large group health plans provide coverage for mental health care in the same manner that they provide coverage for physical health care, such as surgical and medical benefits. For example, this act prevents an employer's group health plan from placing a lower lifetime limit on mental health benefits than the plan's lifetime limit on surgical and medical benefits.

This act applies to employers with more than fifty employees, as long as compliance with the act will not increase the employer's cost by at least one percent. It is important to note that this act does not require large group health plans to include mental health coverage in the benefits that they offer. The law only applies to large group health plans that already include mental health benefits in their packages.

Family Medical Leave Act (1993)

The **Family Medical Leave Act** (**FMLA**) was passed to allow eligible employees to take up to twelve weeks of job-protected, unpaid leave during a twelve-month period for specific family and medical reasons. Employees are covered under this act if their employer has at least fifty employees—full- or part-time—working within 75 miles of a given workplace and if they have worked for their employer for at least twelve months and for a total of 1,250 hours over the past year.

FMLA covers leave for the following reasons:

- The birth of a child, adoption, or foster-care placement
- The serious health condition of a spouse, child, or parent
- The serious health condition of the employee, one requiring inpatient care or continuing treatment by a healthcare provider
- Qualifying exigency leave, or leave to address the most common issues that arise when an employee's spouse, child, or parent is on active duty or call to active duty status—e.g., making financial and legal arrangements or arranging for alternative childcare
- Military caregiver leave or leave to care for a covered service member, such as the employee's spouse, child, parent, or his/her next of kin, with a serious injury or illness. Employees are to be granted up to twenty-six weeks of job-protected, unpaid leave during a twelve-month period to care for a covered service member.

Instead of taking all of their leave at once, employees can choose to take FMLA leave intermittently or in blocks of time for specific, qualifying reasons as approved by their employer. One reason for doing so would be for an employee to attend medical appointments for his/her ongoing treatment and testing for a serious health condition.

Spouses who work for the same employer must share the amount of FMLA time they take for the birth of a child, adoption, or foster care placement or for the serious health condition of a child or parent. The total amount of leave taken by both spouses must add up to twelve weeks for the reasons stated above or twenty-six weeks for the care of a covered service member.

Employers also have the right to require employees to take unpaid FMLA leave concurrent with any relevant paid leave, such as sick time or vacation time, to which the employees are entitled under their current policies. In addition, a week containing a holiday still counts as a full week of FMLA, whether or not the holiday is considered to be paid time.

Employers are required to maintain an employee's group health care coverage while they are out on FMLA leave when the employee was covered under such a plan prior to leave. Once an employee's FMLA leave has ended, they are to be reinstated to their original job or to an equivalent job with equivalent conditions of employment, pay, and benefits.

Employers who fail to comply with the FMLA act may face both civil and criminal penalties. Also, if the Department of Labor finds that an employer did not post FMLA rights and responsibilities notices in the workplace, then a penalty of $110 can be assessed for willful failure to post.

Uniform Services Employment and Reemployment Rights Act (1994)

This law was passed to protect the employment, reemployment, and retention rights of civilian employees who serve in uniformed services, veterans, and members of the Reserve. The act requires covered employees to provide their employers with at least thirty days' notice of their need for leave, if possible, and covers them for up to five years of unpaid leave.

Under the Fair Labor Standards Act, exempt employees must be paid their full salary while out on leave (see 29 C.F.R. §541.602), less any compensation that they receive for serving in the military (§541.603). Employees who are out on military leave are also expected to receive the same seniority-based benefits that they would have received had they not been out of work on leave, such as vacation time and 401(k) contributions.

Additionally, if an employee's military leave will be less than one month, an employer must continue healthcare coverage under the same terms as if the employee was still actively employed. After the first month of military leave, employers are not required to continue group healthcare coverage at their expense. Instead, employers can make healthcare coverage available at the employee's expense for a period of twenty-four months or the duration of their military service, whichever is less. Employers are also not allowed to count an employee's military leave as a break in service for pension plan purposes.

The act requires covered employees returning from leave to apply for reemployment within a specific timeframe following completion of their military service:

- If an employee has been out on leave less than thirty-one days, he or she must return to work on the first workday following completion of military service.
- If an employee has been out on leave between thirty-one and 180 days, he or she must apply for reemployment within fourteen days of completing military service.
- If an employee's leave has been in excess of 180 days, he or she must apply for reemployment within ninety days of completing military service.

An employee returning from military leave is to be reinstated to a position that he or she would have been in if not out of work on leave, which may require some retraining efforts on the part of the employer. If after some period of time and retraining efforts, the employee is found not to be qualified for the new position, the employee can return to the position that he or she held prior to military leave.

Under this act, employers are also encouraged to make reasonable efforts to accommodate disabled veterans returning from military leave. Such individuals have up to two years after completing their military service to apply for reemployment.

Employers who fail to comply with USERRA may face both civil and criminal penalties, ultimately repaying any wronged employees for backpay and lost benefits.

Old Age, Survivor, and Disability Insurance (OASDI) Program

The **Social Security Act** (**SSA**) of 1935 designed this program to ensure a continuation of income for individuals who are retired, spouses, and dependent children of employees who are deceased, and individuals who qualify for social security disability. This OASDI program is funded by contributions made by both employees and employers.

At a minimum, employees must work at least forty quarters or ten years to qualify for this program. A surviving spouse or dependent child's eligibility is determined by the length of time the spouse or parent has worked. The amount of benefits paid out to individuals who qualify is dependent upon the length of time the employee worked and the amount they paid into the program.

The majority of payments under this program are made in the category of Old-Age benefits. Individuals who qualify must be at least 62 years of age to receive partial benefits and between 65 and 67 years of age to receive full benefits, depending on the year they were born. In most cases, a non-working spouse can expect to receive half of the amount of benefits of the working spouse.

Individuals who qualify for Social Security disability and receive benefits under this program must prove that they are unable to perform profitable work because they are totally disabled.

Federal-State Unemployment Insurance Program

Unemployment Insurance was created under the Social Security Act (SSA) of 1935 as a way to provide partial income replacement for a period of time to individuals who find themselves unemployed involuntarily. This benefit is funded primarily by employers—via a state unemployment tax—and administered by the individual states under national guidelines.

The number of weeks for which an employee can receive unemployment benefits can range from one to 39 weeks, with 26 weeks being the most common duration. During some periods of high unemployment, the period of 26 weeks can be extended up to an additional 13 weeks.

Eligibility in most states is contingent upon an employee having worked a minimum number of weeks, not being terminated for misconduct, not having left their job voluntarily, not finding him or herself unemployed due to a labor dispute, being available and actively seeking work, and not refusing suitable employment.

Medicare (1965)

This program is an amendment to the Social Security Act (SSA) of 1935 with the purpose of providing healthcare for individuals age 65 and older, which are not dependent on their income or ability to pay. Some individuals under the age of 65 who are disabled, as well as those individuals suffering from end-stage renal disease, are also eligible for coverage under Medicare. The program is funded by employees and employers paying a percentage of salaries.

Medicare has four distinct parts:

- **Medicare Part A** is hospital insurance, which is considered mandatory, and most individuals do not have to pay for this coverage.
- **Medicare Part B** is medical insurance and covers such healthcare expenses as physicians' services and outpatient care. Medicare Part B is optional, and most individuals pay a monthly fee to have this coverage.

- **Medicare Part C** is referred to as Medicare Advantage Plans, such as HMOs or PPOs that are offered by private companies and approved by Medicare. The Medicare Advantage Plans are available to individuals who are entitled to Medicare Part A and enrolled in Medicare Part B. These plans provide participants with hospital and medical coverage, as well as with additional coverage, such as dental, vision, and hearing, and, in some cases, prescription drug coverage. Medicare Advantage Plans can provide substantial cost savings for individuals who are eligible to enroll in them once a year, during an open enrollment period.

- **Medicare Part D** is prescription drug coverage and is considered optional. Individuals who choose Part D pay a monthly fee to have this coverage. Part D is available to individuals who are entitled to Medicare Part A and enrolled in Medicare Part B.

Government-Mandated, Government-Provided, and Voluntary Benefit Approaches

Compensation and benefits can be an essential element in retaining employees and attracting new candidates. Retaining current employees avoids the additional time and costs associated with training a new candidate altogether, as well as the risk of losing any clients or customers the individual may take along when they exit the organization.

Competitive salary and wages can be important in recruiting and retaining staff. However, unless the difference in salary is significant, it is usually not a factor—especially if the overall compensation package value is comparable. A lower take-home pay paired with a wider selection of healthcare and retirement plans may allow a company to offer a better long-term financial plan to its workers. Bonuses are yet another technique for employers to compensate and reward worthy employees.

Benefits can also assist in retention while saving the company money. Voluntary benefits help employees save money by utilizing group discounts with no added cost to the business. Retention of employees is possible with benefits such as health insurance, because many employees would not be able to afford having medical insurance if they exited their companies.

Benefit Programs

Employee benefits fall into two categories: discretionary and non-discretionary.

Non-Discretionary Benefits

Non-discretionary benefits are those benefits that employers are mandated to provide based on certain statutes. These benefits include social security, Medicare, workers' compensation, unemployment insurance, unpaid family medical leave (based on FMLA), and continuation of healthcare coverage (based on COBRA).

Discretionary Benefits

Discretionary benefits are not mandated by law. Employers choose to provide these benefits in order to attract, motivate, and retain their workforce. Discretionary benefits fall into three main categories: health and wellness, deferred compensation, and work-life equity.

- **Health and wellness benefits** include all aspects of healthcare coverage that employers offer, such as major medical plans, dental and vision plans, prescription drug coverage, addiction and substance abuse programs, employee assistance programs (EAPs), wellness programs, and disability/life insurance.
- **Deferred compensation** includes the various types of retirement plans that employers offer, where income is realized at a later date as compensation for work that is performed at the present time.
- **Discretionary benefits** that fall under the category of work-life equity help employees to manage their work schedules with their personal commitments, paid time off for holidays, short-term illness, vacation, jury duty, and bereavement, along with flexible work schedules and telecommuting options. Some employers provide additional discretionary benefits that fall into this category, such as on-site childcare, tuition reimbursement, and relocation assistance.

Health and Welfare

Employers are moving towards consumer-directed healthcare in an effort to keep costs manageable. This simply means making employees responsible for how they spend their healthcare dollars, with the goal of smarter choices.

A direct outcome of this has been the evolution of high-deductible health plans. These plans do not pay for medical services until employees have first paid a very steep out-of-pocket amount, which can be close to a $2,500 deductible for an individual plan and a $5,000 deductible for a family plan. In an effort to help employees offset their costs, high-deductible health plans are often coupled with either a health savings account (HSA) or a health reimbursement arrangement.

- A **health savings account** (**HSA**) allows employees to pay for approved healthcare expenses pre-tax up to the contribution limits that are set by the IRS. Employers may also make contributions to these accounts, and any remaining balances roll over to the next calendar year, are portable, and can be used into retirement.
- A **health reimbursement arrangement** (**HRA**) is an employer-funded medical plan that reimburses employees only for eligible healthcare expenses. Each employee receives an employer-paid contribution that is treated as a benefit, not as compensation. Employees can roll over any unpaid funds into the next calendar year, but the funds are not portable.

Managed Care Plans

Managed care plans are healthcare plans that seek to ensure that the treatments an individual receives are medically necessary and performed in a cost-effective manner. There are several different types of managed care plans:

Health Maintenance Organization

A **health maintenance organization** (**HMO**) is structured to emphasize preventative care and cost containment. Under this plan, physicians are paid on a per-head basis, rather than for actual treatment. Employees covered under an HMO must seek treatment by physicians who are under the HMO contract.

Preferred Provider Organization

A **preferred provider organization** (**PPO**) is formed by an employer who negotiates discounted fees with networks of healthcare providers. In return, the employer guarantees a certain volume of patients. Individuals enrolled in a PPO can elect to receive treatment outside of the network, but they will pay higher copayments or deductibles for doing so.

Point-of-Service Organization

A **point-of-service organization** (**POS**) is a combination of a PPO & HMO that provides direct access to specialists.

Exclusive Provider Organization

An **exclusive provider organization** (**EPO**) is a plan in which the participants must use the providers who are in the network of coverage or no payment will be made.

Flexible Benefit Plans

Flexible benefit plans—under section 125 of the Internal Revenue Code—allow employers and employees to save taxes on the money they pay toward their group-sponsored health and dental plans, as well as on out-of-pocket medical expenses.

Flexible Spending Accounts

Flexible spending accounts (**FSAs**) allow employees to use pretax dollars to pay for approved, out-of-pocket healthcare expenses that are not covered by insurance and dependent-care expenses. This increases employees' take-home pay while decreasing employer payroll taxes, since Social Security (FICA) payroll taxes are lowered.

Each employee determines the amount of pay to have deposited into their FSA account each month during the year. Unpaid funds cannot be rolled over into the next calendar year, so the money is commonly referred to as "use it or lose it." However, if the employee decides to leave their company prior to the end of the year before contributing the full dollar amount of a claim that was previously paid by the company, they cannot be held responsible for the remaining balance of the claim.

Full Cafeteria Plans

Full cafeteria plans—under section 125—allow employees to choose from a menu of eligible, qualified healthcare benefits and typically pay for them with pre-allocated benefit credits. Some plans permit employees to cash out any unused benefit credits or to buy additional benefits through pretax salary reductions. Full cafeteria plans allow employees to choose the benefits that are most important to them and their families.

Dental and Vision Insurance

Dental and vision insurance are additional health and wellness benefits frequently provided by employers. Dental and vision plans often stress preventive care, and it is common practice to have employees share in paying a portion of plan premiums.

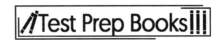

Life Insurance
Life insurance is another health and wellness benefit typically provided by employers. In the event of an employee's death, the surviving family members will normally receive anywhere from one to two times the employee's annual salary as payment. Some companies allow their employees to purchase life insurance in addition to what they provide.

Disability Insurance
Disability insurance is provided by employers as a health and wellness benefit.

- **Short-term disability insurance** pays an employee a percentage of their salary—typically 50 percent to 70 percent—after a brief waiting period. This is in the event that they are unable to work for a short period of time—normally between 10 and 26 weeks—following a non-work-related injury or illness.
- **Long-term disability insurance** takes over when an employee is still unable to return to work after being out on short-term disability. Long-term disability insurance pays an employee a percentage of their salary—typically 50 to 60 percent—until he or she can return to work or for the number of years listed in the company's policy.

Wellness
Corporate wellness programs are gaining in popularity and are used to maintain and improve employees' health before serious problems arise, in an effort to offset the rising costs of healthcare. Often companies kick off these programs by having their employees participate in voluntary health risk assessments and biometric screenings, testing for such things as blood pressure, body mass index, and cholesterol/blood glucose levels.

Based on employees' individual scores, they can be referred to participate in various wellness workshops—e.g., cardiovascular disease prevention, diabetes prevention, healthy aging, nutritional counseling, or understanding back pain—and/or personalized coaching in order to bring about healthy changes. Employee participation in a wellness program is often tied to an incentive, such as a specific dollar amount taken off of their healthcare premiums, in order to create a change in behavior. Employers directly benefit from employee participation in wellness programs through decreased absenteeism, improved productivity, and decreased spending on healthcare and workers' compensation.

Retirement
In **defined benefit plans**, employers agree to provide employees with a retirement benefit amount based on a formula. There are different approaches to this formula:

Flat-Dollar Approach
Plans using a **flat-dollar approach** pay a set dollar amount for each year of service under the plan. This is usually seen in plans covering hourly employees under a collective bargaining agreement.

Career Average
Plans utilizing a **career average** have two methods of computing their formula. In the first method, an employee earns a percentage of pay for each year they are a plan participant. In the second method, an employee's yearly earnings are totaled and then averaged over the number of years they are in the plan. At retirement, the benefit equals a percentage of the career average pay multiplied by the employee's years of service.

Final Pay Approach

Plans using a **final pay approach** base their benefits on the average earnings during a specified number of years—usually towards the end of an individual's employment.

Cash Balance Plans

Cash balance plans are a specific type of defined benefit plan. These plans express the promised benefit in terms of a hypothetical account balance. They are easily communicated to plan participants, and the accrued benefit is portable. Each year, a participant's account is credited with two types of credits:

- Pay credit: equates to a percentage of their compensation
- Interest credit: a fixed or variable rate linked to an index, such as U.S. Treasury bills

Defined Benefit Plans

Some advantages of defined benefit plans are that the benefit is known to the employee, and the employer bears the burden of the financial risk. However, the cost is unknown. These plans tend to create higher rewards for longer-tenured employees.

Defined Contribution Plans

In **defined contribution plans**, employees and/or employers pay a specific amount into the plans for each participant. Employer contributions are often based upon a percentage of salary or a percentage of profits. Performance of the funds in these plans ultimately determines employees' benefits.

Examples of defined contribution plans are 401(k) plans, where the yearly amount employees can put into the plan is set by the IRS and adjusted annually for inflation. 403(b) plans are similar in nature and set aside for employees of certain tax-exempt organizations, such as K–12 public schools, colleges and universities, hospitals, libraries, churches, and philanthropic organizations. Additionally, profit-sharing plans are yet another example of this type of plan.

Some advantages of defined contribution plans are that they can provide valuable benefits to employees with less service and the cost is known. However, the benefit is unknown, and the employee bears the burden of the financial risk.

Here's a breakdown:

Characteristics Of Defined Benefit And Defined Contribution Plans Advantages

	Defined Benefit Plan	Defined Contribution Plan
Employer Contributions and/or Matching Contributions	Employer funded. Federal rules set amounts that employers must contribute to plans in an effort to ensure that plans have enough money to pay benefits when due. There are penalties for failing to meet these requirements.	There is no requirement that the employer contribute, except in SIMPLE and safe harbor 401(k)s, money purchase plans, SIMPLE IRAs, and SEPs. The employer may have to contribute in certain automatic enrollment 401(k) plans. The employer may choose to match a portion of the employee's contributions or to contribute without employee contributions. In some plans, employer contributions may be in the form of employer stock.
Employee Contributions	Generally, employees do not contribute to these plans.	Many plans require the employee to contribute in order for an account to be established.
Managing the Investment	Plan officials manage the investment and the employer is responsible for ensuring that the amount it has put in the plan plus investment earnings will be enough to pay the promised benefit.	The employee often is responsible for managing the investment of his or her account, choosing from investment options offered by the plan. In some plans, plan officials are responsible for investing all the plan's assets.
Amount of Benefits Paid Upon Retirement	A promised benefit is based on a formula in the plan, often using a combination of the employee's age, years worked for the employer, and/or salary.	The benefit depends on contributions made by the employee and/or the employer, performance of the account's investments, and fees charged to the account.
Type of Retirement Benefit Payments	Traditionally, these plans pay the retiree monthly annuity payments that continue for life. Plans may offer other payment options.	The retiree may transfer the account balance into an individual retirement account (IRA) from which the retiree withdraws money, or may receive it as a lump sum payment. Some plans also offer monthly payments through an annuity.
Guarantee of Benefits	The Federal Government, through the Pension Benefit Guaranty Corporation (PBGC), guarantees some amount of benefits.	No Federal guarantee of benefits.
Leaving the Company Before Retirement Age	If an employee leaves after vesting in a benefit but before the plan's retirement age, the benefit generally stays with the plan until the employee files a claim for it at retirement. Some defined benefit plans offer early retirement options.	The employee may transfer the account balance to an individual retirement account (IRA) or, in some cases, another employer plan, where it can continue to grow based on investment earnings. The employee also may take the balance out of the plan, but will owe taxes and possibly penalties, thus reducing retirement income. Plans may cash out small accounts.

Stock Purchase

Employee stock plans are another tool that companies can use to incentivize employees by making them think and behave as owners in the company. A stock option plan affords employees the opportunity to purchase a fixed number of shares of the company's stock at a fixed, or exercise price, during a certain period of time. Employees hope to buy the shares of the company's stock when those shares are trading at a price higher than the exercise price, which will lead to a profit.

An **employee stock ownership plan (ESOP)** is an example of a qualified defined contribution retirement plan that is a stock bonus program. ESOPs give employees significant stock ownership in their companies and allow them to benefit from any associated profitability and growth, which can motivate them to be more focused on the performance of their organizations. Although ESOPs can provide valuable benefits, the employees bear the burden of the financial risk.

Employee Assistance Programs (EAPs)

These are employer-sponsored benefit programs that are used to provide help for employees who are experiencing difficulties in the areas of anxiety, depression, marital or family relationship problems, legal issues, and financial concerns. These programs assist employees with identifying their problems with short-term interventions. For instance, employees may be referred to an expert for assistance with complex matters. Employees' use of EAPs is voluntary and confidential, and employers typically provide this service by contracting with a counseling agency.

Payroll Processes

Payroll is responsible for numerous processes that occur on various schedules and at different times throughout the year. Running the standard paycheck cycle is a regular and frequent process that is done according to the organization's pay schedule. Whether weekly, bi-monthly, or monthly, payroll must ensure that time is tracked accurately and approved by the appropriate supervisor. Time off must be audited to ensure the appropriate leave is reported and any new accrued leave is added to the employee's balances.

If errors are made, it is important for payroll to review and audit the issue, make the necessary corrections, and establish a process to ensure the error does not occur in the future. Payroll may need to issue a check outside of the normal pay schedule and an established process should be followed in these cases. When an employee resigns or is terminated, checks must be issued within specific timeframes to ensure compliance with state laws. Ensuring a process to issue these off-cycle is established and followed is important for any payroll function.

In addition to the standard pay schedule processing, payroll is also responsible for ensuring that annual W-2 tax forms are prepared, printed, and mailed to all employees who worked for any period of time in the previous year. This includes individuals that contracted with the organization as well as employees and can be a quite cumbersome process. The W-2 form must be sent to all individuals no later than January 31 of the following year (ex. 2017 W-2 forms must be sent by January 31, 2018) per federal IRS guidelines. Additionally, a 1095 schedule must be prepared to report the status of healthcare insurance of the employee and all dependents during the year to abide by the guidelines in the Affordable Care Act.

In addition to the above standard processes, Payroll is responsible for ensuring that employee's compensation is accurate. If back-pay is required, Payroll must calculate what is owed and ensure the employee receives this compensation as soon as possible. If a promotion is not entered in a timely manner, or a merit increase is delayed, Payroll is responsible for retroactively calculating this new rate for all the paychecks missed. Payroll is also responsible for working with auditors to ensure appropriate processes are established and followed, necessary checks and balances are put in place, and all general accounting practices are understood and incorporated into policy, practice, and procedure.

Salary and Benefits Surveys

A **salary and benefit survey** is an excellent tool that organizations can use to determine the appropriate salary for a job, benchmark wages against the market, and make decisions about benefits. Surveys should incorporate all compensation data, including salary, retirement benefits, healthcare benefits, time off, and any other form of compensation to ensure that a holistic view is available. Establishing the surveys can help provide insight regarding attrition, or why employees are leaving the organization, as well as recruitment difficulties, or why candidates are not wanting to join the organization. Various surveys are available for the private sector in specific geographic areas as well as specific to certain industries. Organizations can then compare the compensation and benefits offered against the market to determine if adjustments or corrections are necessary. These are characteristics of an effective salary and benefits survey:

- Representative of the market and region
- Inclusive of multiple positions at various levels
- Low cost
- Convenient and easy to navigate
- Precise and accurate information

These are characteristics of an inadequate salary and benefit survey:

- Has inflexible design, reporting only statistics
- Does not address controversial issues
- May not reflect comparable industries

It is important to understand all the pros and cons when using a salary and benefits survey, specifically that the data may not hold all the answers. There may not be comparable positions or data points for every position in the organization, so various degrees of extrapolation may be necessary. This can be potentially contentious if an individual believes they are not paid a fair wage and is requesting an increase. Regardless, having the data is an important step in understanding how the organization compares with competitors and the marketplace. While a survey may not answer all of an organization's questions, it can provide insight and when used properly, an effective tool.

Claims Processing Requirements

Organizations should ensure that the process for filing a claim is clear, concise, and fully understood by all employees. Employees should know what they need to do and when. Supervisors should also know what they need to do and when in the case that one of their employees is injured. Most claims processes require the following steps:

- 1. Employee immediately reports the injury to employer.

- 2. Employee is seen by a doctor immediately, either a physician as identified by the employer, the employee’s primary care physician, or an urgent care facility.

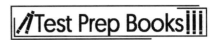

- 3. Claim forms are completed by the employee, including the following information:
    - Date and time of injury
    - Witnesses, if any
    - Specific details of the injury including body part(s) and damage
    - Specific details of how the injury occurred
- 4. Claim forms are reviewed by the supervisor, with the supervisor adding additional information if necessary.
- 5. Claim forms and medical reports are returned to the administrator of the program.
- 6. The administrator reviews the claim and reports and file with the insurance adjustor.
- 7. If the employee is to be off of work to recover, HR communicates with supervisor about the timeframe for time off.
- 8. If the employee is to return to work with restrictions, HR communicates the restrictions to the supervisor and determines if the organization can accommodate the employee.
- 9. If accommodations cannot be made to return the employee to work, the employee is placed on leave pending new restrictions or a return to work.
- 10. Prior to returning to full duty, employees have a follow-up review with the physician who will determine when the return to full duty can occur.

While the above is a sample process, it is vital to ensure that your organization's procedures, forms, and requirements are frequently communicated to employees. Employees should understand their responsibilities in reporting injuries and which actions need to occur and when. Employees should know where to locate the forms and who the main administrator of the program is. They should also be aware of their rights and of the resources available to them. If a claim has been rejected, employees should understand their appeal rights and how to request a review of the rejected claim.

After a worker's compensation claim has been initiated, it is vital that an organization review the incident and what occurred. After this review has been completed, the organization should take action, if appropriate, to ensure that the injury does not occur again in the future. This could include additional training, new safety equipment, or a change in a process. Organizations that are proactive in safety measures are less likely to have injuries and workers compensation claims.

Work-Life Balance

Work-life balance is a goal for everyone. Organizations that promote flexibility and balance generally have happy, engaged, and motivated employees. Organizations should constantly look for new ways to incorporate flexible practices in the workplace. Employees appreciate and are grateful for the opportunity to balance life and work by incorporating these practices into their lives. Some common best practices for work-life balance are:

- Flexible work schedules (4 x 10 or 9 x 80 workweek)
- Telecommuting or work-at-home options
- Reduced work schedules such as part-time work
- Reduced overtime
- Onsite child care and child-friendly policies
- Relaxed dress code policies and programs
- Approving extended leaves of absences to accomplish outside goals

It is important to understand that what one employee values may not be important to another employee. Having a variety of programs available can help to ensure that there is something for everyone. It is also important to understand that work-life balance does not mean an equal balance. Depending on the position, operations, customer needs, and organizational requirements, flexibility may not be available at certain times. Flexibility in work schedules may be available only at certain times of the year, depending on the industry and the needs of the company.

Additionally, as an employee's personal situation changes, their needs may also change. Single employees with no children will have a different definition of work-life balance than a married employee with five children. While it is impossible to provide a program that satisfies every single employee, it is possible to have various programs that align with the business and potential needs of individuals. A best practice to incorporate into an organization is to establish employee surveys and focus groups to hear directly from many employees what programs would increase work-life balance. There may be possible solutions and recommendations that can be researched and implemented. Not only is a new program available, but employees will be more engaged and motivated because they were involved in the process.

When employees have a healthy work-life balance, employers see an increase in focus, motivation, and job satisfaction. Additionally, employers see higher productivity levels and less negativity and stress in the work environment. Employees are generally healthier and less stressed, and they accomplish their work goals. Additionally, employees have healthier relationships outside of work. The work culture is one of engagement, motivation, and high morale. Employees know they are valued, supported, and important to the success of the organization.

Practice Questions

1. The federal minimum wage is currently set at $7.25/hour. However, in the state of Maryland, where Rachel's ice cream parlor resides, the minimum wage is currently set somewhat higher at $8.25/hour. Which statement below accurately reflects the rate of pay at which Rachel's new employees starting out at the minimum wage would receive?
   - a. The new employees will receive $7.25/hour. When the federal minimum wage is set lower than a state's minimum wage, an employer can go with the lower rate of pay as its standard.
   - b. The new employees will receive $8.25/hour. When a state's minimum wage is higher than the federal minimum wage, an employer must use the higher state minimum wage as its standard.
   - c. The new employees will receive $7.75/hour, which is an average of the federal minimum wage and the state's minimum wage.
   - d. Rachel's ice cream parlor does not have enough employees to fall under the guidelines of the Fair Labor Standards Act (FLSA), which governs minimum wage.

2. Which of the following individuals would qualify for non-exempt status under the Fair Labor Standards Act (FLSA)?
   - a. An employee whose position does not require specialized education
   - b. An individual who supervises the work of two or more staff members
   - c. An employee who must use independent judgment in their daily work
   - d. An employee who earns more than $455 per week

3. Which of the following is NOT one of the three categories that the IRS's twenty factors fall under for determining if an individual working at a company is an employee or an independent contractor?
   - a. Financial control
   - b. Reporting accountability
   - c. Behavioral control
   - d. Type of relationship

4. Which of the following items is NOT a covered provision under the Fair Labor Standards Act (FLSA)?
   - a. Overtime pay
   - b. Employee classification
   - c. Child labor
   - d. Hazard pay

5. Which piece of legislation requires employers to pay employees for preliminary and postliminary tasks, such as job-related travel time that is outside of an employee's regular work commute and time spent in job-related training?
   - a. Equal Pay Act
   - b. Portal-to-Portal Act
   - c. Fair Labor Standards Act (FLSA)
   - d. Davis Bacon Act

6. Which of the following statements is true regarding differential pay?
   a. Differential pay is required by the Fair Labor Standards Act (FLSA).
   b. Differential pay programs are used to reward employees for performing work that is viewed as less than desirable.
   c. Pay practices regarding differential pay are standardized among employers.
   d. Differential pay programs are used to motivate employees to perform their work at a higher level.

7. A pension plan that meets the minimum standards set by the Employee Retirement Income Security Act (ERISA) must do which one of the following?
   a. Allow new hires to participate beginning in their first month of employment
   b. Provide plan participants with a copy of the summary plan description once every ten years
   c. Include schedules for graded and cliff vesting
   d. Allow the employer to keep pension plan assets together with other company assets

8. What is the compa-ratio for a salary range of $10–$22 and an entry-level employee salary of $12.50?
   a. The compa-ratio is 70 percent.
   b. The compa-ratio is 78 percent.
   c. The compa-ratio is 1.04 percent.
   d. The compa-ratio is .96 percent.

9. Based on the compa-ratio determined by the previous question, which of the following can be deduced about the employee and/or the company's pay strategy?
   a. The employee is new to the job and/or the organization, is a low performer, or is working for a company that has adopted a lag behind the market pay strategy.
   b. The employee is new to the job and/or the organization, is a high performer, or is working for a company that has adopted a lag behind the market pay strategy.
   c. The employee is long-tenured, a high performer, or is working for a company that has adopted a lead ahead of the market pay strategy.
   d. The employee is long-tenured, a low performer, or is working for a company that has adopted a lead ahead of the market pay strategy.

10. An employee has passed away on the job. For what length of time is his surviving wife eligible for continuation of healthcare coverage under the Consolidated Omnibus Budget Reconciliation Act (COBRA)?
   a. Three months
   b. Eighteen months
   c. Thirty-six months
   d. Twenty-nine months

11. Considering they have met all of the necessary requirements, which of the following individuals is eligible to take unpaid, protected leave from work under the Family Medical Leave Act (FMLA)?
   a. An employee who is non-weight bearing, recovering from ankle surgery, and who will have multiple follow-up appointments with his surgeon and numerous physical therapy visits to attend.
   b. An employee who is out of the office for three days sick with the flu.
   c. An employee who wants to take care of her aunt who is suffering from end-stage lung cancer.
   d. An employee who wishes to travel to China to support her sister who is in the process of adopting a child in that country.

12. Which of the following benefits is considered to be discretionary?
   a. Unpaid family medical leave
   b. Life insurance
   c. Continuation of healthcare coverage
   d. Worker's compensation

13. Which of the following is considered to be indirect compensation?
   a. Bonus
   b. Incentive pay
   c. Pension plan
   d. Hourly wage

14. Which of the following is used to describe the knowledge, skills, abilities, education, and experience that are essential to performing a specific job?
   a. Job analysis
   b. Job description
   c. Job specification
   d. Job evaluation

15. Which of the following is a quantitative method of job evaluation?
   a. Job ranking
   b. Paired comparison
   c. Factor comparison method
   d. Job classification

16. Once a salary survey is completed, what is the term used for weighting the data for jobs included on the survey that are similar, but not identical, to positions with the organization? This process is done to create a more accurate match.
   a. Aging
   b. Benchmarking
   c. Leveling
   d. Wage compression

17. Which of the following is a direct result of broadbanding?
   a. Green-circle rates below pay structure
   b. Taller organizational structures
   c. Red-circle rates above pay structure
   d. Flatter organizational structures

18. Which of the following types of compensation is given to employees when they work during holidays or vacation days?
   a. Reporting pay
   b. Shift pay
   c. Premium pay
   d. Emergency shift pay

83%

Answer Explanations

1. B: The new employees at Rachel's ice cream parlor will receive $8.25/hr. When a state's minimum wage is set at a higher rate than the federal minimum wage, such as Maryland's minimum wage, an employer must use the higher state minimum wage as its standard when paying employees.

2. A: Employees who qualify for non-exempt status under the Fair Labor Standards Act (FLSA) are those who earn a salary of less than $23,600 per year or $455 per week, do not supervise others, and whose positions do not require specialized education or the use of independent judgment.

3. B: The three categories that the IRS's twenty factors fall under for determining if an individual working at a company is an employee or an independent contractor are Choice *A*, financial control, Choice *C*, behavioral control, and Choice *D*, type of relationship. Reporting ability is not one of the categories.

4. D: Hazard pay is not a covered provision. The Fair Labor Standards Act (FLSA) establishes guidelines around Choice *A*, overtime pay, Choice *B*, employee classification (exempt and non-exempt status), minimum wage, on-call pay, record keeping, and Choice *C*, child labor.

5. B: The Portal-to-Portal Act deals with the preliminary and postliminary tasks of employees. The act requires employers to pay employees who are covered under the FLSA for time spent traveling to perform job-related tasks, if that travel is outside of the employees' regular work commute. Additionally, employees are to be paid for hours spent in job-related training that is outside of their normal workday.

6. B: Differential pay programs are used to reward employees for performing work that is viewed as less than desirable, and these programs vary greatly among employers. Differential pay is not required by the FLSA.

7. C: The plan must include minimum vesting schedules for graded and cliff vesting. In order for a pension plan to meet the minimum standards set by ERISA, employees must be at least twenty-one years of age and have completed one year of service with the company in order to participate in the plan. Plan participants must be provided with a copy of the summary plan description at least once every five years. Additionally, the pension plan assets must be kept separate from other company assets.

8. B: The compa-ratio is computed by finding the mid-point of the salary range, which is $16 in this example. Then, the pay level of the employee ($12.50) is divided by the midpoint of the salary range ($16) to receive a compa-ratio of .78 or 78 percent.

9. A: Since the compa-ratio in question eight is 78 percent and, thus, below 100 percent, the employee is paid less than the midpoint of the salary range. This can be attributed to the fact that the employee is new to the job and/or the organization, is a low performer, or is working for a company that has adopted a lag behind the market pay strategy.

10. C: Thirty-six months is the period of eligibility under COBRA for a divorce/legal separation or death of an employed spouse, as well as for a dependent child who loses eligibility status under the plan rules. Eighteen months is the period of eligibility under COBRA for an employee's reduction in hours or an employee's termination. Twenty-nine months is the period of eligibility under COBRA for the disablement of an employee.

11. A: FMLA only covers unpaid, protected leave for the following reasons:

- The birth of a child, adoption or foster-care placement
- The serious health condition of a spouse, child, or parent
- The serious health condition of the employee
- Military caregiver leave, or leave to care for a covered service member with a serious injury or illness

Employees are to be granted up to 26 weeks of job-protected, unpaid leave during a 12-month period to care for a covered service member.

12. B: Life insurance is a discretionary or voluntary benefit that is provided by employers. Choice *A*, unpaid family leave (based on FMLA), Choice *C*, continuation of healthcare coverage (based on COBRA), and Choice *D*, worker's compensation, are all non-discretionary benefits, since employers are mandated to provide them based on certain statutes.

13. C: Pension plan. Indirect compensation, most commonly referred to as employee benefits, includes such elements as healthcare coverage, retirement/pension plans, paid time off from work, and short-term and long-term disability.

14. C: Job specification is the knowledge, skills, abilities, education, and experience that are essential to performing a specific job. Choice *A*, job analysis, is the process used to identify the particular job requirements and duties and their relative importance. Choice *B*, job description, is a general written statement for a specific position based on a job analysis. Choice *D*, job evaluation, determines the relative worth of each job position by creating a hierarchy.

15. C: Factor comparison method. Quantitative job evaluation methods use a scaling system and provide a score that indicates how valuable one job is when compared to another job. The two specific examples noted are the point factor method and the factor comparison method. Choice *A*, job ranking, is when an organization defines the value of a specific job compared to other jobs in the organization. Choice *B*, paired comparison, is when an individual and their position is compared to another individual and their position. Choice *D*, job classification, is a system designed to evaluate the duties and authority levels of a job.

16. C: Leveling can be used if a job included on a salary survey is similar, but not identical, to a position within the organization. The data for that job can be weighted or leveled to create a better match. Choice *B*, benchmarking, is used to evaluate something by using a comparison. Choice *D*, wage compression, is when a new employee is paid at a higher wage than an individual who is currently employed in a similar position and with similar skills.

17. D: Broadbanding leads to flatter organization structures. Broadbanding occurs when employers decide to combine multiple pay levels into one, which results in only a handful of salary grades with much wider ranges. This type of pay structure is easier to administer and eliminates green and red circle rates. Broadbanding also leads to a flatter organizational structure, which encourages employees' horizontal movement through skill acquisition versus the traditional vertical movement through promotions to new pay grades.

18. C: Premium pay can be given to compensate employees as a higher rate of overtime pay for working on holidays or vacation days. Some employees receive shift pay, Choice *B*, for working second or third shifts or for being called into work during an emergency, also known as emergency shift pay, Choice *D*. Reporting pay, Choice *A*, can be paid to employees who arrive at their place of employment and find that there is no available work for them to perform.

Human Resource Development and Retention

Laws and Regulations Related to Training and Development Activities

Copyright Act of 1976

The **Copyright Act of 1976** is the foundational law in the United States regarding property ownership of film, radio, musical and dramatic works, literary and pictorial works, and architectural structures. Superseding local and state copyright laws, the statute establishes a standardized and universally applied measure to the country's major social and technological transformations in media. Hitherto the act, there were deficient authorship protections that had the capacity to safeguard creative works and lawfully secure remunerative rewards. Written with a broad intent, the landmark legislation is applicable to "original works of authorship fixed in any tangible medium of expression."

In order to lawfully reproduce, disseminate, modify, publicly display, or perform copyrighted material, one must hold a copyright over such material, published or unpublished. Stipulated by the Copyright Act of 1976, a copyright lasts for the duration of the author's life, plus an additional seventy years after his or her death. However, the law incorporates a policy of "fair use." Fair use enumerates some instances in which a person may use copyrighted material.

Fair Use

The Copyright Act of 1976 specifies instances in which protected material can be used without threat of infringement. These selective requirements fall into the jurisdiction of "fair use." The first qualification is the intended purpose of the work. Is it intended for commercial gain or for non-profit education? Secondly, fair use is determined by the nature or type of work in question. Thirdly, the amount or proportion of the copyrighted work is evaluated. Lastly, the potential variation in market value of copyrighted material is determined. Educational purposes, research, criticism, scholarship, comment, teaching, or news reporting are the categories specifically noted that would determine the applicability of fair use.

Public Domain

When any of the works delineated have no copyright, they enter into the public domain. In the public domain, any person can use these works freely. In order for a work to not be protected by federal copyright law, it needs to meet one of two conditions. If the federal government publishes the work, it is regarded as public, and therefore is exempt from copyright infringement. Expiration is the only other way an article would lose copyright protection. Works created on or after January 1, 1978, are protected for the life of the author and seventy years after his or her death; anonymous works, works-made-for-hire, and articles are protected for ninety-five years from the date of creation or 120 years after being published. Works-made-for-hire includes works made by employees or works that are specially ordered or commissioned.

Title 17

Title 17 is a United States copyright law enacted in 1947. It applies to authorship of any tangible medium of expression. Specific works that fall under Title 17 are literary works, architectural works, musical recordings, pictures and graphics, choreographic works, musical works, motion pictures, and audio works.

U.S. Patent Act

The **U.S. Patent Act** expressly prohibits the unauthorized use, sale, reproduction, or distribution of the product without the consent of the patent holder. The legislation's broad composition is designed to preserve and protect the property of inventors. Furthermore, one of two conditions must be met in order for protections to be granted by the act to apply: the invention in question must be created in the United States or the invention must be imported into the country. Although the law explains several prohibitions regarding the unsanctioned use, sale, reproduction, or distribution of an invention, it does not specify any legal recourse in the event of infringement of a particular patent.

Patent Types

There are three types of patents in the United States: utility, design, and plant. The most common type of patent is a utility patent. A **utility patent** involves anything technological, mechanical, chemical, pharmaceutical, or software-related. Utility patents are valid for twenty years after the date the patent is filed. In order to obtain a utility patent, one must provide a written and meticulously detailed description of the product. The second type of patent is a **design patent**. These patents are valid for fourteen years after the date they are filed. Unique to the United States, this patent comprises ornamental design –specifically, the way a product looks (aesthetics) and how it actually works. For instance, when applying for a design patent for a bookcase, the inventor must exhibit how it is assembled, how much weight it can withstand, and the size screws that must be used to give it requisite support. A **plant patent** can be filed for an asexually reproducible plant discovered in a cultivated area. These patents last for twenty years after the date they are filed. Plant patents are the least common type of patent.

Trademark Act

The **Trademark Act** was created to provide for the protection and registration of trademarks and service marks.

Title VII

Title VII is a federal law within the Civil Rights Act of 1964. It stipulates that no person shall be discriminated against on the basis of sex, race, color, national origin, and religion. Although Title VII is a federal law, it applies to state and local governments as well. Moreover, the law applies to private and public colleges and universities, private sector employment, and labor unions. Under this law, all employees are guaranteed equal access to career development and training.

Training Delivery Format

There are two primary formats of training delivery: on-the-job training and off-the-job training. **On-the-job training** refers to training that is specifically done while observing or doing the actual job. This can include receiving instruction, shadowing, observing, and rotating with other employees to learn a wide variety of skills. **Off-the-job training** refers to training that occurs away from the job. This can include attending a classroom session or lecture, watching webinars or online tutorials, or attending a conference. Regardless of the format and delivery of the training, all training is important to the success of an employee achieving their individual goals and the organization achieving their strategic objectives. Regardless of the delivery format, training programs should always work to include multiple types of learning methods to ensure that employees are able to absorb, understand, and use the material provided.

In general, on-the-job training incorporates learning methods that relate directly to the work that an employee will be performing. Hands-on experience is sometimes the best training for an employee, depending on the work. On-the-job training can be used when job shadowing or cross-training employees to learn additional skills and operations.

Off-the-job training is just as important and provides learning opportunities in a different way for different topics. Learning how to function as a team, communicate better, and resolve conflicts are common topics that are best taught in a classroom setting. Additionally, training employees on policy, procedure, ethics, diversity, harassment, and other important subject matter is best taught in a focused classroom setting with a knowledgeable and interactive instructor.

When selecting the best method of training, employers should choose the method that enables employees to be completely focused on the subject they are learning. To teach an employee how to properly and safely use a drill press, on-the-job training is most likely the best option. If the training is to teach an employee how to report injuries, learn new communication techniques, or file a complaint regarding safety or harassment issues, off-the-job training is most likely the best option. In some cases, it may be beneficial to incorporate both training formats to ensure maximum success in learning the material. This type of hybrid training program may incorporate an hour of classroom training to review standards, protocols, safety procedures, and textbook operations before heading out to the field to receive on-the-job training with the actual machinery at the worksite. Training delivery should always be selected based on the specific subject matter.

Evaluating Training Programs

Training programs are a great way to enhance employee's knowledge, skills, and abilities related to their work efficiency and effectiveness. It is important though to ensure that the programs are evaluated to ensure they are effective and employees are using the information and skills learned. The primary principles of training evaluations are to:

- Ensure training objectives and goals are clear and understood
- Provide specific areas for improvement, enhancement, or additional ideas for discussion
- Enable evaluation of the trainer and overall effectiveness in presenting the material
- Enable evaluation of the materials and resources provided
- Provide realistic target dates and follow up evaluations for the training information

There are numerous methods that can be used to determine the effectiveness of a training program, and each program or class should have an evaluation method that is appropriate to the training material. For example, training courses that are administered for mandatory education in topics such as corporate policy, sexual harassment legislation, or discriminatory practices may require a training evaluation that reviews employee's understanding of the material and recommendations for future courses. Training courses that teach employees how to be an effective supervisor and provide tools and resources to use in everyday situations should have evaluations that do the following:

- Assess the effectiveness of the training course immediately at the conclusion
- Assess the effectiveness of the new tools and resources 30 days after training
- Assess the effectiveness of the new tools and resources 6 months after training
- Determine which tools are being used and making a difference in the workplace

If the evaluations show that the participants are not really using the information presented in the training course, it may be useful to reassess how the participants are selected for the training program. Ensuring the participants are those who need and will use the information is vital to ensuring a successful training program. The best training programs will not be successful if the right employees are not identified to participate.

Training programs should be reviewed frequently to ensure that the material is the most recent, up-to-date information available. New learning methods are constantly being created and training courses should reflect various learning methods to ensure that all employees are engaged and involved in the learning opportunities. Individuals all learn in different ways, so it is important that instructors incorporate various learning techniques into the training programs. Asking employees to assess this during the evaluation can help determine whether the techniques were effective.

Career Development Practices

Career development encompasses six primary stages: assessment, investigation, preparation, commitment, retention, and transition. Career development is an important process when attempting to make a person attractive to prospective employers. During the assessment stage, a person begins to realize that he or she is unsure about his or her values, weaknesses, interests, and strengths. This stage requires a conscious effort on behalf of the person to begin an exploration process. In the investigation phase, a person begins to search for opportunities that the world of work has to offer. After the investigation stage, a person has acquired knowledge about what best suits him or her and begins preparation. The commitment stage comes after a person recognizes his or her talents, prompting a commitment to a particular job or career. After a person feels most comfortable in his or her career, he or she begins to sharpen his or her skills and become acclimated with his or her industry—this is the retention stage. Lastly, the transition stage forces a person to assess his or her happiness and make connections to a new career (if necessary).

In addition to career development, there are other ways that enable a person to advance his or her career. Other methods include support programs, employee counseling, training workshops, and coaching programs. **Support programs**, which attempt to remedy personal and utility problems, create channels for employers to assist employees who are not maximizing their potential with training or counseling. Similarly, to support programs, employee counseling is an institutional program used by employers to maximize productivity within the organizational structure. Training workshops enable employers and employees to identify particular skills and ensure that they are placed in a position of maximum utility. Coaching workshops place workers under the supervision of a counselor in order to equip them with the tools to solve problems that may be inhibiting their work capacities.

In order to create an environment that allows all workers to maximize their potential in an organizational structure, employers offer programs that are designed to benefit the career development of employees. A few of these methods are evaluating, mentoring, counseling, and coaching. A proper evaluation of the deficiencies, skills, and psychological health of employees is important to identify their strengths and weaknesses, while determining their most efficient roles in the organization. Mentoring programs for employees is a critical component to making sure that they are under guardianship at a professional and emotional level. Counseling in the workplace permits employees to be given additional personal and professional support. Under the supervision of professional counselors, workshops that offer coaching to employees can bolster both organizational and personal health.

Over the course of their careers, individuals often use various methods to enrich their careers. Some of these methods include networking, pursuing supplementary formal education, and attending training workshops. Networking permits individuals to build beneficial connections with people who may be able to help them obtain employment. At networking events, an individual will attempt to speak to as many people as possible to establish relationships. When job searching, individuals may discover that many opportunities require more skills than they possess. To remedy this problem, many people pursue additional education to make them more marketable and attractive to prospective employers. Training workshops are events designated to let individuals discover their skills, allowing them to pursue careers that correspond to them.

Retention

After taking the necessary time to recruit the right employees, it is important for companies to work to retain them. Employee turnover has high costs associated with it—lost time and lost productivity. There are many different ways that companies attempt to retain staff, and not one method works for all employees. For example, some employers feel that offering a competitive benefits package that includes health care, a retirement program, and life insurance is the best way to retain employees. However, sometimes low or no cost options that improve employees' work/life balance, such as flextime, telecommuting, and allowing employees to wear jeans to work every day (unless they are attending customer-facing meetings) are the best way to go. In addition, staff can be grateful for, and tend to stay longer at, workplaces that provide perks that are meaningful to them, such as on-site childcare, tuition reimbursement, dry cleaning pickup, and free doughnuts on Fridays.

Employers can stay in touch with how their employees are feeling about the work environment by conducting what is known as **stay interviews**. During these interviews, topics including why employees came to work for the employer, why the employees have stayed at the employer, what would make the employees consider leaving, and what the employees would want to see changed are discussed. This allows management to make necessary improvements before they find themselves conducting exit interviews.

Finally, in a workplace that is serious about retention, open communication between management and employees about the company's mission and future goals is key. It is also important for management to show concern for employees' continued development and to promote from within when possible.

Performance Appraisal Methods

Performance appraisal is a process that is integral to maintaining standards that are essential to consistent productivity in an organization. An intricate process, performance appraisal measures and evaluates the quality of work that is performed by employees. It is a barometer by which employees must exceed pre-established benchmarks and simultaneously uphold organizational protocol. Moreover, managers and administrators compare performance appraisal results with other employees and expectations while making rational decisions regarding efficacy and value. From the process, management crafts a compilation of results and data with the intention of performing a cost-benefit analysis. After these analytical methodologies are conducted, management and administrators will enact appropriate changes for improvement.

After a performance appraisal, management will affect these improvements through incentivizing programs. Increasing salaries or rewarding promotions are typically two strategies that are used to reinforce desired behavior. For employees who are found to be less efficient or productive, training or counseling programs are a means of providing underperforming individuals with the tools to improve. In some instances, management will pursue punitive responses to underperformance: demotions, reductions in pay, or termination of employment. Essential to performance appraisal is the establishment of firm standards and procedures for an organization in which underperformance will be quickly rectified. An inflexible organizational infrastructure forces employees to conform to the institution, rather than institutional codes being disregarded and ignored.

Communicational development is a crucial advantage of performance appraisal. A channel of communication is clearly delineated through two principal means: organizational rules and regulations, and explicit managerial examinations. Organizational policies offer nonverbal guidance to employees by consistently challenging them to assimilate to protocol while sustaining maximal productive capacities. After performance appraisals are conducted, managerial expectations can be developed, and solutions to remedy underperformance can be pursued. Any disputes between labor and management can quickly be softened by maintaining stringent channels of communication, where both sides have assigned responsibilities and coordinate to meet shared goals.

Ranking/Rating Scales

A system for rating employees is the **behaviorally anchored rating scales**, or **BARS**. BARS is a unique system because it specifically focuses on behaviors that are necessary for performing a task successfully, rather than evaluating more analytical employee habits. Instead of appraising general behaviors that are required to be present in all employees, BARS examines precise behaviors that are unique to a certain job or task. After an investigation has taken place, management will employ a designated rating scale that appropriately locates an employee based on performance. On the rating scale, a "1" designates unsatisfactory performance, a "2" designates marginal performance (troublesome employees), a "3" designates fully competent performance, a "4" designates excellent performance, and a "5" designates exceptional performance.

The 1–5 rating scale method demonstrated above is just one of the numerous varieties. In addition to the 1–5 rating scale, they can also express a 1–3 model, 1–4 model, 1–5 model, or 1–10 model. These models are known as rating scale methods. Moreover, another prominent method of appraisal is the checklist method. The **checklist method** features a series of questions that determine a specific level of performance, with the participant placing a check next to applicable statements.

Relationship to Compensation

Rating is a tactic that employers use to incentivize employees to efficiently fulfill tasks in a timely manner. In addition, rating is a way that employers can measure and identify their productive, talented, and best workers. After employees are rated, the highest-performing individuals will be rewarded. Similarly to rating, rewarding is a mechanism used to incentivize and reinforce positive behavior. In all successful organizations, employers have discovered the most efficient means of regulating, monitoring, and sculpting maximal performance strategies.

Training for Evaluators

One key reason why performance appraisals tend to be ineffective is that most individuals who evaluate employee performance have received little or no training on how to do so, and they are not adequately supported throughout the performance appraisal process.

Therefore, many types of performance appraisal errors may result. Evaluators make the similar-to-me error when they rate employees more favorably who are like themselves. Contrast errors come into play when an evaluator focuses on a particular stereotype, such as age or race, instead of on performance when rating employees, or when an evaluator compares two employees who have similar performance records and rates one of the employees higher than the other due to his or her likeability. Excessive leniency or excessive strictness occurs when performance appraisals are written to be too accommodating or too harsh and tend to be more about the evaluator's temperament than about the employee's job performance. The halo effect takes place when an employee receives a glowing performance appraisal (is rated highly in all areas regardless of actual job performance), after the evaluator notices that he or she is really very good at performing one aspect of his/her job (perhaps something that the evaluator values personally).

The opposite of halo effect is what is known as the horn effect. The horn effect takes place when an employee receives a negative performance appraisal (is rated poorly in all areas regardless of actual job performance), after the evaluator notices that he or she is poor at performing one aspect of his/her job (perhaps something that the evaluator values personally). In addition, central tendency error takes place when the evaluator gives all employees a middle of the range performance appraisal score (i.e., a 6 out of 10), so he or she cannot be perceived as "the bad guy" if the truth about employees' job performance is told. The recency effect takes place when an evaluator bases an employee's performance appraisal solely on a recent event (good or bad) instead of on the employee's entire performance history during the established rating period. The opposite of this is what is known as the primacy error. This error takes place when an evaluator bases an employee's performance appraisal solely on his or her initial impression of the employee (good or bad) instead of on the employee's performance history during the established rating period.

Evaluators should receive the necessary training to ensure that employees' performance appraisals are free from all bias and discrimination. This involves training on how to use the performance tool, training on the various types of performance appraisal errors listed above and how to avoid them, along with how to manage difficult conversations with employees. Performance appraisals should be based on formal evaluation criteria that has been previously set and on evaluators' personal interactions with the employees. Evaluators should accurately describe employees' behavior by citing specific examples using objective criteria and to document situations as they occur. Additionally, equitable treatment should be provided to all employees during the performance appraisal process.

Outcomes of Performance Management Programs

There are several outcomes of the performance management process, including:

- Disciplinary actions that can be taken for underperforming employees
- Pay increases and incentive rewards
- Opportunities for employee advancement and promotions
- Employee development plans
- Career/succession planning

Performance management gives organizations the opportunity to identify the most suitable jobs for the most qualified people. After analyzing the results of goal setting, if certain individuals possess skill sets that indicate that they would be more productive in other areas of the business, this phase allows those transitions, or transfer assignments, to occur. Furthermore, promotions can be used to reinforce positive behavior. Another strategic use of promotions is to maximize each individual's utility by encouraging them to take positions that they may not have otherwise been interested in. These types of employment moves should be properly documented through the employees' performance appraisals to ensure that the organization is protected should any legal concerns arise.

Performance Management Practices

Goal Setting

A robust system of planning can be incorporated into an organization's agenda to set expectations and devise strategies to meet them. Monitoring performance levels enables organizations to ensure that operations harmonize with expectations. If specific goals are not met, this indicates an error in planning or execution. Identifying any unmet goals makes organizations more likely to become more productive by constantly improving.

Benchmarking

Employers use salary surveys to assist them when working to establish the pay structures for their organizations. These surveys collect information from multiple employers regarding salary and benefits, such as employees' starting salaries, merit increases, bonus amounts, and work hours. In order to be comparable, salary surveys are conducted by focusing on a specific geographic region or industry.

Employers can make use of free government salary surveys and inexpensive industry-specific salary surveys, such as those for civil engineering and construction. Employer associations, like the **Society for Human Resource Management** (**SHRM**), also conduct salary surveys and provide the results to their members at no charge. Additionally, companies can elect to outsource a salary survey to a survey vendor, which can be quite pricey.

It is important to note that salary survey data contains time-sensitive data that can become outdated rather quickly. Salary data may also need to be aged and/or leveled. **Aging** is the process of adjusting salary data to keep pace with market movement. **Leveling** can be used if a job included on the salary survey is similar—but not identical—to a position within the organization. The data for that job can be weighted or leveled to create a better match.

Instruments

Some types of performance appraisals are the 360-degree feedback, general appraisal, employee self-assessment appraisal, and the technological/administrative performance appraisal. The 360-degree feedback method is a way for employees to receive feedback about their performance in an anonymous manner from individuals they frequently work in close contact with, such as their managers, peers, direct reports, customers, and suppliers. The employee self-assessment appraisal forces employees to examine their own work, while management conducts a concurrent appraisal. After these are completed, the two are jointly compared. The technological/administrative performance appraisal concentrates on employees who perform technical jobs. The type of work they do, productivity levels, output, and other important tasks are barometers by which employers measure.

Practice Questions

1. What is the purpose of a pilot program?
   a. The purpose of a pilot program is to assign leadership and decision-making roles to a program, designating leaders as "pilots."
   b. The purpose of a pilot program is to function as a test program, in which leadership conducts analyses to assess the program's feasibility and revenue-wielding potential.
   c. The purpose of a pilot program is to rescue a pre-existing project from certain failure.
   d. The purpose of a pilot program is to validate the success of a project by awarding higher salaries and bonuses to leadership.

2. One of the six stages of career development is assessment. What occurs during this stage?
   a. The assessment stage demands that people assess their new occupation and begin working on assignments.
   b. The assessment stage requires that people begin looking for opportunities that reflect their interests and skills.
   c. The assessment stage occurs when people begin to feel a comfort and familiarity with their careers and become acclimated.
   d. Assessment is an introspective stage that requires that one be aware of their values, interests, and skills to discover a career that is most suitable.

3. Kinesthetic learning is accomplished most efficiently through which of the following?
   a. Kinesthetic learning is learning that is done by listening to lectures or group discussions.
   b. Also called spatial learning, kinesthetic learning is learning that is best done by watching videos, looking at maps, or copying notes from a blackboard.
   c. Kinesthetic learning is learning that takes place through physical touching or moving. Examples of kinesthetic learning are using building blocks or drawing.
   d. Kinesthetic learning is learning that is best done by reading text and writing down an alternate interpretation of that text.

4. What does a plateau learning curve indicate?
   a. A plateau learning curve represents initially slow learning but then a rapid acceleration.
   b. A plateau learning curve indicates quick initial learning followed by a stoppage.
   c. A plateau learning curve indicates sluggish learning, acceleration in learning activity, and then a deceleration.
   d. A plateau learning curve represents quick initial learning followed by a slowdown.

5. What are the three types of organization development interventions?
   a. Human process intervention, sociotechnical intervention, techno-structural intervention
   b. Human process intervention, managerial intervention, techno-structural intervention
   c. Managerial intervention, human process intervention, techno-structural intervention
   d. Employer intervention, sociotechnical intervention, techno-structural intervention

6. Which statement is most reflective of the Pareto analysis system?
   a. 20 percent of output is generated by 80 percent of input.
   b. 80 percent of output is generated by 20 percent of input.
   c. Decisions should be made democratically rather than statistically.
   d. Resources need to be allocated according to need rather than according to productivity.

7. Which is a primary principle of DRIFT?
   a. One primary purpose of DRIFT is to distribute high profits to employees so that they will be more loyal.
   b. One primary purpose of DRIFT states that as long as they are dealt with immediately, errors can be tolerated.
   c. One primary purpose of DRIFT is that stockpiling commodities can be profitable because supplies are easily accessible.
   d. One primary purpose of DRIFT is that supply and demand must be congruent with management expectations.

8. Public domain is a copyright provision that posits which of the following?
   a. Under no circumstances can a previously copyrighted work be used without authorization.
   b. Any work published by the federal government can be used freely without authorization.
   c. Items that are considered to be works-made-for-hire never fall into the public domain.
   d. Works protected by a copyright can be used without consent if they are used for a public purpose.

9. Which of the following pieces of legislation guarantee that all employees have equal access to career development and training?
   a. Title VII of the Civil Rights Act of 1964
   b. Fair Labor Standards Act (FLSA)
   c. Older Workers Benefit Protection Act (OWBPA)
   d. Davis Beacon Act

10. Which of the following statements is true regarding a learner analysis in the needs assessment process?
   a. Data is gathered from both mid-level and senior level managers.
   b. It will ensure the company is on board with the training.
   c. It can be completed in conjunction with the task analysis.
   d. Data is gathered from individuals who have direct knowledge of the work.

11. Which of the following best represents 360-degree feedback?
   a. A method by which employees receive anonymous feedback from their managers, peers, direct reports, and customers.
   b. A method by which employees perform a self-appraisal regarding their own performance at several different points over the course of a year.
   c. 360-degree feedback features reviews only by fellow employees. This is most effective because learning how employees interact with each other is indicative of their attitudes and efforts.
   d. 360-degree feedback uses reviews only by management. Only management can assess an employee's suitability in an organization by evaluating productivity levels.

12. In performance management, what is a principle function of rating?
   a. Rating allows management to identify their most productive workers and provide them incentives to retain them.
   b. Because of its narrow statistical application, rating is generally an infrequent practice by management.
   c. To provide a way for management to designate their most favored employees.
   d. By employees rating management, they can more accurately decide for whom and under which conditions they wish to work.

13. Peter Senge postulated that there are five disciplines that complete a learning organization. When appropriately used in an organization, what is the purpose of these disciplines?
   a. The purpose of Peter Senge's five disciplines is to permit an organization to function more comprehensively by augmenting communication and establishing common goals.
   b. The purpose of Peter Senge's five disciplines is to articulate management's exact expectations to employees.
   c. The purpose of Peter Senge's five disciplines is for employees to compete for the best ideas and to incorporate them into a productive strategy.
   d. The purpose of Peter Senge's five disciplines is discovering different modes of innovation and to force employees to conform to them without engaging in dialogue.

14. Which of the following accurately represents the Fishbone Diagram?
   a. The Fishbone Diagram is centered on the analysis of management and does not consult the entire organization.
   b. The Fishbone Diagram identifies the effects and works to determine causes.
   c. The Fishbone Diagram investigates the causes of problems. It is crafted after comprehensive brainstorming, determines positive and negative consequences, and isolates various components.
   d. The Fishbone Diagram is a way to provide a visual representation of a distribution of data.

15. Which of the following best represents the purpose of Six Sigma?
   a. Six Sigma is a rationally motivated and methodological process that seeks to eliminate ineffective and wasteful techniques that diminish productivity.
   b. Six Sigma is a process that seeks to terminate wasteful programs through organizing management and employee councils.
   c. The major purpose of Six Sigma is to use brainstorming techniques to gain valuable feedback from employees to determine the most ineffective use of company resources.
   d. To increase productive capacities, organizations employ Six Sigma. Six Sigma recruits employees with the most experience, not necessarily the most highly trained in Six Sigma methodology or statistics.

Answer Explanations

1. B: Also known as an experimental trial or feasibility study, a pilot program is designed to be small-scale. A pilot program's purpose is to enable an organization to test new methods, new products, or engineer new methods or techniques without incurring significant cost. Tremendously important to research, pilot programs can be considered laboratories of innovation and experimentation because they allow logistical considerations, structural efficiencies and deficiencies, and profitability to be evaluated and determined. Pilot programs are widely used in application by many companies, notably Microsoft Corporation, Pfizer Inc., The Dow Chemical Company, and Xerox Corporation.

2. D: Assessment is the first stage of career development. This stage asks that an individual do soul-searching. It demands that a person discover their values, interests, skills, and passions in order to find a career that is most suitable. It can be seen as a stage of self-affirmation that precedes the journey of job searching. During this stage, a person may ask: "What inspires me?" and "What is my purpose?" Assessment is unique to the other stages of career development because it is independent and exists outside of the workplace.

3. C: Kinesthetic learning can most easily be described as learning by doing. Whereas auditory learning occurs by listening, visual learning occurs through sight, and reading/writing learning occurs through interacting with text, kinesthetic learning occurs distinctly through touch and movement. Kinesthetic learners may grasp concepts more easily by physical activity, such as playing sports, laboratory exercises, drawing, charades, building, or role-play. To properly accommodate kinesthetic learners, one may use field trips, memory games, or flash cards. Studying while loud music is playing, poor penmanship and spelling, inability to sit still for long periods of time, and emphasis on breaks while studying are a few of the signs of a kinesthetic learner.

4. B: A learning curve is a graphical representation of a person's learning progress. A plateau learning curve indicates that learning takes place at an accelerated rate and then comes to a halt. Out of the four types of learning curves discussed, the plateau learning curve is unique. It is the only learning curve that indicates a stoppage in learning. A positively accelerating learning curve represents slow initial learning, but then a rapid increase. A negatively accelerating learning curve depicts an accelerated beginning followed by a slowdown. Lastly, an S-shaped learning curve denotes initial sluggishness, heightened learning activity, followed by a return to lethargy.

5. A: The three types of organization development interventions are human process interventions, sociotechnical interventions, and techno-structural interventions. Human process interventions are coordinated efforts to correct inefficiencies through human contact. Specific types of human process interventions are coaching, mentoring, training, or using a third party to mediate disputes. Sociotechnical interventions attempt to integrate new machinery and technology into pre-existing organizational models. Lastly, the goal of techno-structural interventions is to use technology to its most productive capacities.

6. B: The Pareto analysis system is a statistical model that postulates that 80 percent of output is generated by 20 percent of input. Management can use this rule to identify where to invest scarce resources. Other names for this rule are the "80-20 rule" and "law of the vital few." Remembering these other names can be helpful because they highlight the essential functionality of the rule. By constantly searching for the most productive members of an organization or the resources that yield the most revenue, management personnel are able to prioritize employees or investments over others. This analysis can be useful when restructuring an organization, rating employee performance, capital investment, and much more.

7. D: DRIFT is a technique that organizations adopt to harmonize supply and demand. In practice, DRIFT can only be successful if the costs of production are in accordance with expectations. Just-in-time is a concept that is accompanied with DRIFT. In order to control the costs of stockpiling unused wares, long-term and close-knit relationships with suppliers and creditors are imperative. If an organization did not have easy access to supplier and financial institutions, then its ability to respond to the vacillations of the market would not be as swift.

8. B: Public domain is a provision in federal copyright law stating that work that meets designated criterion can be used without authorization. There are two possibilities where one can use material without obtaining consent. First, if the federal government publishes a work, then it is considered to be public, thus falling into the public domain. Second, copyrights can expire. Material that is created on or after January 1, 1978 is protected for the remainder of the author's life plus seventy years after death. Anonymous material, works made for hire, and articles are protected for ninety-five years from the date of creation or 120 years after being published.

9. A: Title VII of the Civil Rights Act of 1964 guarantees that all employees have equal access to career development and training. The Fair Labor Standards Act (FLSA) was put into effect to establish employee classification (exempt/non-exempt) and regulate minimum wage, overtime pay, on-call pay, associated recordkeeping, and child labor. Under the Older Workers Benefit Protection Act (OWBPA) it is illegal for employers to discriminate based on an employee's age in the provision of benefits, such as pension programs, retirement plans, life insurance, etc. Finally, the Davis Beacon Act requires contractors and subcontractors working on federally funded contracts in excess of $2,000 to pay all laborers at construction sites associated with such contracts at least the prevailing wage and fringe benefits that individuals working in similar projects in the area are receiving.

10. C: A learner analysis can be completed in conjunction with a task analysis during the needs assessment process. Data is gathered from both mid-level and senior level managers during an organizational analysis, and the point of performing this type of analysis is to ensure that the company is on board with the training. Data is gathered from individuals who have direct knowledge of the work during a task analysis.

11. A: 360-degree feedback is a method by which employees receive anonymous feedback from their managers, peers, direct reports, and customers. Choice *B* is incorrect since 360-degree feedback involves much more than employee self-appraisals. Choice *C* is incorrect since 360-degree feedback involves much more than reviews by only fellow employees. Choice *D* is also incorrect since 360-degree feedback involves much more than reviews only by management.

12. A: There are multiple functions for rating in performance management. The first purpose of rating is to give management the opportunity to identify the best performing employees. Once this is done, these employees can be rewarded in various ways. Conversely, rating is a technique used by management to distinguish poorly performing employees. Underperforming employees can be dealt with in many ways: they can receive a decrease in pay, be forced to attend additional training programs, or ultimately have their employment terminated.

13. A: The intended purpose of the five disciplines outlined by Peter Senge is to enable organizational apparatuses to remain adaptable and capable of change. Essential to the five disciplines are communication, dialogue, team learning, and establishing common goals. Individuals must develop personal skills and mastery, but there remains an equal focus on the organization itself. It must be able to adapt to extemporaneous circumstances, adopt innovative tactics, and embrace participatory approaches that permit the fluidity of ideas. By compelling members of an organization to communicate and work cooperatively, the concept of systems thinking is critical to Senge's five principles.

14. C: The Fishbone Diagram is a tool that seeks to analyze the primary causes of an effect of a problem. Ultimately, the diagram engages problems and investigates remedial efforts for improvement. In a group formation, a consensus is gathered to identify possible causes, which could range from employee performance or outdated technology to inefficient methods of production or environmental implications. By isolating each factor, the diagram details organizational procedure to scientifically diagnose potential inefficiencies.

15. A: Six Sigma is a method used by organizations to reduce inefficiencies and other cumbersome techniques that diminish profitability. It is a rationally organized process that is enlisted to constantly increase productive capacities by eliminating antiquated or outdated machinery and technology. Furthermore, Six Sigma may scrutinize opaque bureaucratic structures or wasteful practices that obstruct maximum profitability. Grounded in statistical analysis, this methodology exhibits a scientific and technical approach to solving critical problems facing an organization.

Employee Relations

Laws Affecting Employment in Union and Nonunion Environments

WARN Act

The **Worker Adjustment and Retraining Notification** (**WARN**) Act of 1988 requires that a minimum of 60 days' notice be given in advance of plant closings and mass layoffs. The notice must be given to local government, state dislocated worker units, and workers or their representatives. This piece of legislation applies to employers with one hundred or more full-time employees, or employers who have a total of full-time and part-time employees working 4,000 hours per week (not counting overtime) at all of their employment sites combined. A plant closing is the temporary or permanent shutdown of an entire site or one or more facilities or operating units within a single site that results in an employment loss during any thirty-day period of 50 or more full-time employees. A mass layoff is a reduction in force (not a plant closing) during any thirty-day period that results in an employment loss at a single site for either 50 or more full-time employees, if they make up at least 33 percent of the workforce at the employment site, or 500 or more full-time employees. Employment loss is the involuntary termination of employment (other than for cause), layoff for more than six months, or at least a 50 percent reduction in hours for each month of a six-month period.

The WARN Act provides for three situations in which the sixty-day notice is not required, but the burden is on the employer to show that the reasons are legitimate and not an attempt to thwart the intent of the act. First, the "faltering company" exception applies only to plant closures in situations where the company is actively seeking additional funding and has a reasonable expectation that it will be forthcoming in an amount sufficient to preclude the layoff or closure, and that giving the notice would negatively impact the ability of the company to obtain the funding. The "unforeseeable business circumstance" exception applies to plant closings and mass layoffs and occurs when circumstances take a sudden and unexpected negative change that could not have reasonably been predicted. Finally, the "natural disaster" exception applies to both plant closings and mass layoffs occurring as the result of a natural disaster such as a tornado, earthquake, or hurricane.

National Labor Relations Act (Wagner Act)

Passed in 1935, the **National Labor Relations Act** (**NLRA**) grants specific rights to workers who already belong to, or wish to join, a union. In addition to reinforcing the rights covered by the Norris-LaGuardia Act, this piece of legislation also grants employees the right to participate in collective bargaining activities, even if they are not a member of the union in question. There are some restrictions, however, such as the NLRA does not affect the special restrictions of the Railway Labor Act. In addition, the NLRA does not affect certain individuals who may make decisions on behalf of an employer, such as managers, supervisors, independent contractors, and immediate family.

The NLRA also defines what constitutes a legal and an illegal strike. A strike is considered legal when employees are seeking a better work environment, benefits, or compensation, or when an employer is using an unfair labor practice. A strike is considered illegal when employees have signed a contract with a no-strike clause, employees are striking to defend a union's unfair labor practice, or there is a significant concern that the striking employees are expected to cause property damage or bodily harm.

The NLRA also dictates what can be considered unfair labor practices, such as an employer doing one or more of the following: stopping workers from joining or participating in a union, taking control of a union or showing favoritism to any particular union, discriminating against union participants, discriminating against a worker who has filed charges with the National Labor Relations Board (NLRB), and refusing to bargain with the union representing its employees.

In addition, the NLRA created the National Labor Relations Board (NLRB) to encourage union growth. This board is primarily responsible for investigating potential unfair labor practices. The NLRB focuses on protecting employees from unfair treatment by employers or unions. The NLRB has the authority to take various actions to combat unfair labor practices, including the following: forcing employers to rehire employees, forcing employers to negotiate with a union, disbanding employer-controlled unions, forcing unions to refund excessive membership fees, forcing unions to negotiate with an employer, and forcing unions to reinstate members.

Employee and Employer Rights and Responsibilities

Employment-At-Will

Employment-at-will refers to the employment of employees who do not have a contract indicating the terms of employment and who can be discharged by an employer at any time for any reason. While there are some legal protections for employees who have filed complaints regarding harassment, discrimination, retaliation, or whistleblowing, in general an at-will employee can be terminated from employment without notice and without cause. The term "cause" in this context refers to actions that are considered violations of policy which could include inappropriate behavior, fraud, misappropriation of funds, untruthfulness, or other actions that would warrant termination. Depending on the organization and its agreements and policies, some employees may be at-will employees and others may have protections established through union representation or other contractual terms.

It is important to remember that employment-at-will does not allow an employer to fire someone at will. Employees still have rights and protections afforded to them under federal and state legislation. Employers must understand how an employment-at-will situation aligns with these protections when considering terminating an employee who has at-will employment status.

Defamation

Defamation refers to intentionally injuring another individual's name or reputation by spreading lies or untruths through slander and/or libel. **Slander** specifically refers to a verbal statement or gesture that defames an individual, and **libel** specifically refers to a written or recorded statement that defames an individual. Regardless of the intention behind defamation, individuals and organizations can be held accountable for their actions when they cause injury to another's reputation. Slander and libel are not protected under the First Amendment, or freedom of speech, and those guilty of defamation are held accountable for their actions. Organizations often deal with defamation in various ways and levels of severity. Rumor mills and gossip chains, regardless of the intention, are common, everyday forms of defamation that can cause stress, poor working relationships, and negative work environments. Many organizations have begun to implement policies that combat gossip to ensure that employees are working in a safe and healthy environment, free from defamation in any form.

Employer/Employee Rights Related to Substance Abuse

Substance abuse is a dependence on an addictive substance such as illegal drugs. This dependency not only impacts the individual but also may affect families and communities. Programs specifically designed to combat substance abuse can be extraordinarily beneficial. Because substance abuse is not limited to adults, programs may be introduced that focus on children and adolescents as well. In addition to the physical dangers of substance abuse, subsequent behavioral patterns compound issues. If treatment is not sought, the likelihood of a life of crime and poverty greatly increases.

Effective substance abuse policies protect both employers and employees in the workplace. Privacy policies generally authorize employers to conduct random drug tests if the employee has given prior consent. The employee should be clearly notified when hired that these tests may be administered by the employer. Employee substance abuse is damaging to the workplace and often results in inappropriate conduct with co-workers, insubordination, and fatal injuries due to improper use of machinery.

Through the Americans with Disabilities Act, federal guidelines exist to protect both employers and employees in regard to substance abuse. Employers do have the right to ensure a drug-free workplace by prohibiting the use of illegal drugs and alcohol. Employers may test for illegal drug use but must meet state requirements to do so. If an employee tests positive for current drug use through proper testing procedures, employers have the right to terminate that employee.

The ADA gives protection to employees who have successfully rehabilitated from past drug use but are no longer engaged in the illegal use of drugs. Employers cannot discriminate against any employee who has either completed a rehabilitation program or is undergoing rehabilitation. Reasonable accommodation efforts should be extended to those individuals who are rehabilitated or are undergoing current treatment.

Ergonomics refers to the ability of a person to fully utilize a product while maintaining maximum safety, efficiency, and comfort. Ergonomic risk factors in the workplace can lead to musculoskeletal disorders such as carpal tunnel, rotator cuff injuries, muscle strains, and lower back injuries. In order to reduce these risks, employers should evaluate workplace ergonomics and educate employees about potential issues. An ergonomic evaluation tests a product to determine its ease of use and potential safety risks. When employers identify and address ergonomic concerns in the workplace, they protect their workers and likely prevent serious injuries.

Collecting Employee Feedback

Employee Attitude Surveys

Employee surveys are a tool that management can use to determine how HR programs are being received by staff, to uncover problem areas in the organization, and to reveal employee preferences or needs. These surveys can be distributed as attitude surveys with the goal of measuring employees' job satisfaction or as opinion surveys with the goal of gathering data on specific issues. It is important that employees know they will be guaranteed anonymity in return for their participation in the survey so they will, in turn, be as honest as possible on how they view their jobs, supervisors, coworkers, organizational policies, etc. This type of employee input provides management with data on the "retention climate" in the company. Collecting this data is extremely important to an organization's retention measurement efforts. It is important for management to share the results of the survey with employees, even if the feedback is negative. By continuing to administer employee surveys annually or at set intervals, management can measure improvements in responses over time.

Focus Groups

Focus groups are small, pre-selected groups of individuals who discuss specific topics in a relaxing environment. Focus groups are an excellent way to gauge employee opinions regarding the employment experience. Topics can include healthcare options, compensation, specific programs, work schedules, training, growth opportunities, supervisory relationships, promotion opportunities, or any other topic that an organization would like direct opinions on from the employees.

It is important to select participants from different departments, different positions, various tenures of service, and various age ranges to ensure diverse perspectives are offered during the focus groups. It may be necessary to have multiple focus groups discussing the same topics to gauge variances or similarities among the individuals in the groups and the groups themselves. When facilitating a focus group, it is vital to ensure that the participants know if the information will be confidential or available to decision makers. Some participants may not be as willing to share information for fear of retribution or retaliation if their comments and opinions are shared with others. If it is possible, removing names may be a best practice to implement to ensure open and honest dialog and feedback. Without this, a focus group may not yield the best information and ultimately not the best use of time or resources.

Exit Interviews

Individuals who are leaving a company are given an exit interview to uncover their reasons for parting ways with the organization. **Exit interviews** are typically conducted by a neutral party, such as an HR professional, rather than by the departing employee's direct supervisor. HR will typically summarize and analyze the data from exit interviews at regular intervals to share information with management regarding possible improvement opportunities.

Workplace Behavior Issues

Various issues can arise in a workplace that must be addressed by HR. It is extremely important to ensure that policies and procedures address as many of these issues as possible so that employees understand expectations and appropriate behavior in the workplace. A common concern that many organizations deal with is absenteeism, the practice of not showing up for work or requesting time away from work, sometimes for dubious reasons. Organizations should have a detailed policy for employees to follow to request time away from work. Vacation leave, sick leave, bereavement, military leave, or other types of leave should be requested and approved by a supervisor before the leave is taken.

Although emergencies happen and an employee may not be able to submit a request for approval prior to taking leave, employees should know how to report these emergencies. This ensures that the organization can plan its workload while the employee is out. If an employee needs to be absent from work due to an illness, the organization should have policies and procedures in place for requesting this leave, especially if it is related to the Family Medical Leave Act or a state-specific illness leave. In some circumstances, employees may be abusing their leave and not following proper procedures to request time off. There may even be occasions where an employee uses certain types of leave fraudulently, such as taking sick leave but going to Disney World and posting pictures on social media. In the cases that an employer suspects an employee of fraudulent use of leave time, an investigation should be conducted and appropriate action taken. Counseling or progressive discipline may be warranted based on the circumstances and the findings of the investigation.

Aggressive behavior, employee conflict, and workplace harassment are all behavior issues that an organization may have to address and resolve appropriately. Regardless of the concern, the first step should be conducting a thorough investigation. The concern may be brought forward through a formal complaint process, or it could be discovered through other means such as having a conversation with an employee or through general knowledge of an incident.

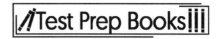

The first step of the resulting investigation should be to interview the individuals involved, including witnesses and supervisors. The second step is to determine what occurred and whether the behavior violated company policy. If there was a violation, the appropriate steps should be taken to hold the individual accountable. Progressive discipline, counseling, training, or even termination may be warranted based on the circumstances of the incident and the egregiousness of the actions.

Afterward, it is important to communicate to the appropriate employees that the matter has been investigated, appropriate actions have been taken, and the matter is now resolved and closed. HR should also review the matter with a holistic lens to determine whether additional training is necessary to ensure that the behavior does not occur again the in the future. It may also be appropriate to communicate the policies, procedures, and expectations to all employees. By being as proactive as possible, employers can work to prevent future occurrences and ensure a safe and engaging workplace free from conflict, harassment, bullying, or other inappropriate behaviors.

Investigating Complaints or Grievances

Grievance Procedures

A **grievance** is a complaint made by an employee that is formally stated in writing. A formal grievance procedure allows management to respond to employee dissatisfaction appropriately through formal communication. Additionally, if a unionized employee is being questioned by management in a situation where a disciplinary action may result, they have the right to union representation during that conversation, which is also known as Weingarten rights (after a famous court case). If that right is violated and the unionized employee is let go, they can be reinstated with back pay.

Every contract will lay out a slightly different process to address potential contract grievances. However, many will follow a similar pattern. The goal is always to remedy the situation before it escalates to the need for arbitration. Typically, employees first discuss the grievance with the union steward and the supervisor. Next, the union steward discusses the grievance with the supervisor's manager and/or the HR manager. The next step is for a committee of union officers to discuss the grievance with the appropriate managers in the company. Then, the national union representative discusses the grievance with designated company executives. If, after this process, the grievance is still not settled, it then goes to arbitration. Grievance arbitration is a process in which a third party is used to settle disputes that arise from conflicting interpretations of a labor contract. Decisions that are reached through this process are enforceable and cannot go to court to be changed.

Settling Discrimination Charges

Unfortunately, discrimination exists in some organizations, and sometimes official charges are brought forth. In these cases (and even in cases where the organization is confident that no wrongdoing has taken place), an organization has a decision to make. It can follow the process through the Equal Employment Opportunity Commission (EEOC) and be investigated by a Fair Employment Practices Agency (FEPA) at the local or state level. Or, the organization may choose to settle the charges rather than face an investigation. Employee charges of discrimination must be filed with the EEOC within 180 days of the alleged incident. If probable cause is found, then the EEOC will attempt conciliation, and the employer is required to settle. The complaint charge is either settled, or the process may move to litigation with either the EEOC or a private court. If the EEOC is not able to determine probable cause, the employee can request a right-to-sue letter after the end of the 180-day period and must file suit in court within ninety days. Finally, if the EEOC does not find probable cause, the employer and employee are both notified. The employee can request a right-to-sue letter, and the EEOC's involvement with the case ends. The employee can then sue the employer in court.

There are a number of factors that can influence a company's decision to settle discrimination charges. One is the financial cost of an investigation. Lawyers and court fees can be a financial strain on a company's finances, not to mention additional obligations if the court rules against the company. There are also the challenges of the investigation itself to consider. If charges are brought to the EEOC or FEPA, a company may be required to devote considerable time and resources to cooperating with the investigation. Thus, an organization may decide that a one-time financial penalty is preferable to an extended period of disruption. A company also faces damage to its reputation. A long, drawn-out trial and investigation, potentially widely covered on social and traditional media, can do irreparable harm to the company's image. Even in cases where the company is found to be blame-free in the case, the general public may still associate the organization with the charges of discrimination. Therefore, a company may find it is better to accept the financial expense to avoid the potential long-term damage to its reputation. Finally, there are systemic problems to think about. If the company is aware of deeper issues of discrimination among its employees, it may choose to settle charges to avoid having the investigation uncover an ongoing pattern that may be hard to address.

Front Pay

If a company is found guilty of workplace discrimination, it is usually required to allow the individual in question to return to their position within the organization. However, in some instances, the court may rule that the company should require front pay. **Front pay** is money awarded to an individual in a workplace discrimination case and is generally equal to lost earnings. Front pay is usually required when the position is not available, the employer has not made any effort to address an ongoing issue of discrimination throughout the company, or the employee would be forced to endure a hostile work environment if they were to return to the original position.

Mediation Process

Mediation often serves as a precursor to the more official step of arbitration. In general terms, arbitration is sometimes thought of as a form of mediation, but legally there are important differences. Most notably, a mediator doesn't serve as a final "judge" of the dispute, but rather attempts to work with both parties to help them reach a resolution without having to take additional legal steps.

The mediation process usually begins with both parties agreeing to use a mutually acceptable mediator. The mediator sets the ground rules for the process and defines details such as what the dispute is about, who is involved, when and where the negotiations will take place, and the negotiation procedure. When the actual meeting takes place, the mediator reiterates the ground rules for the process. Both sides present their case. The mediator attempts to help both parties reach a compromise or find other solutions. If both sides agree to a compromise, a written document will be signed to ensure that both sides will follow through on the agreed-upon actions. If both sides do not agree, they may choose to pursue arbitration or litigation (court action).

Constructive Confrontation

Constructive confrontation is a type of mediation used in some extremely complicated or contentious disputes, particularly ones where neither party is able to agree to a compromise. Constructive confrontation can sometimes break these stalemates by temporarily skipping the main issue in dispute, and instead, focusing first on secondary issues. Sometimes, by first resolving these smaller details, a mediator can affect parties' willingness to compromise on bigger issues.

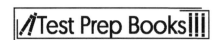

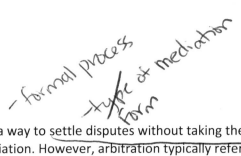

Arbitration

Arbitration is a way to settle disputes without taking the issue to court. In a general sense, arbitration is a form of mediation. However, arbitration typically refers to a more formal process that takes place after an initial mediation attempt has failed. In arbitration, a neutral third party (known as an arbitrator) makes a decision based on the facts presented. There are different kinds of arbitration, decisions, and arbitrators.

In **compulsory arbitration**, the disputing parties are required by law to go through the arbitration process. This could be the result of a court order, but it could also arise from a contract that dictates that arbitration take place in certain situations.

In **voluntary arbitration**, the disputing parties choose to undergo the arbitration process, usually because they cannot come to an agreement, but do not want to go through a potentially expensive and time-consuming lawsuit.

In a **binding decision**, the disputing parties are required by law to follow the decision reached as a result of the arbitration process. This means that the losing party must follow the actions laid out by the decision (such as payments or reinstatement to a disputed position). In addition, a binding decision marks the end of the legal process. No party may pursue further legal action after the decision has been reached.

As the name suggests, **non-binding decisions** carry no legal weight. Either party may choose to follow or not follow the terms of the decision. In addition, a dissatisfied party may choose to follow additional legal action after the decision of the arbiter is reached.

A **permanent arbitrator** is someone who routinely judges arbitration cases for a company or other organization. An arbitrator may be trained and certified by a professional organization, but they also may simply be a person who the disputing parties trust to provide an unbiased opinion on the dispute.

An **ad-hoc arbitrator** may also be a certified professional or a mutually trusted third party. But unlike permanent arbitrators, ad-hoc arbitrators do not have a regular arbitration relationship with either party. Instead, they are chosen as a one-time solution to address only the unique dispute in question.

An **arbitrator panel** functions just like an ad-hoc arbitrator, but it is comprised of multiple arbitrators (usually three). They are sometimes called arbitral tribunals or tripartite arbitration panels.

Progressive Discipline

Warnings

Warnings are the first step in the progressive discipline process. Warnings can be both verbal and written; both are documented so that the discipline history is recorded. Verbal warnings can take the form of informal counseling or discussions to ensure that an employee understands the concern and knows the corrective action to take. At the conclusion of the verbal warning, it is important to ensure that the employee understands what will happen if the behavior is not addressed. Written warnings include official letters or memos documenting the behavior and concerns, with the necessary expectations outlined. Employees should have an opportunity to review the written warning, provide comments, and then sign and date to show a record of receiving the warning. Written warnings should include the specific behavior that is being addressed with the details of the incident: date, time, witnesses, and concerns. Additionally, the policy that was violated should be specifically identified and communicated so that the employee understands why the warning is being issued. Similar to the verbal warning, written warnings should include the expectations of the employee and what will happen if the behavior is not addressed. Written warnings should indicate that progressive discipline, including and up to termination, will be administered if the employee's behavior does not change.

Escalating Corrective Actions

When verbal and written warnings do not address a behavior or performance concern, it may be necessary to escalate to more corrective actions. These actions can include suspensions, or time off without pay, mandatory training programs, demotions, and termination. Organizations are responsible for ensuring their discipline policy outlines the various levels of corrective action. Many agencies have bargaining agreements with their represented employees that require multiple levels of suspension before progressing to termination. Below is an example of an extensive, multi-level escalating progressive discipline schedule:

- Verbal warning
- Written warning
- One-day suspension
- Three-day suspension
- One- week suspension
- Two-week suspension
- One-month suspension
- Termination

Regardless of the length of the schedule, each step should include a documented report indicating the inappropriate behavior or performance, expectations moving forward, the level of discipline being issued for the incident, and what will occur if the behavior does not change or performance does not improve. It may be necessary to conduct a root cause analysis to determine whether additional insight is needed to provide a better course of action to get the employee on the right course. If the discipline is being issued due to poor performance, the primary issue may be training. The individual may be in the wrong position and steps may be necessary to transfer the employee to a more suitable position.

Termination

Termination is the final step in the progressive discipline process and when an employee is removed from their job. Terminations occur for behavioral issues, poor job performance, and policy violations. It is imperative that employees receive sufficient warning regarding the seriousness of their offenses prior to their termination.

Once the decision is made to end a staff member's employment, the actual termination takes place in a swift manner, typically during a face-to-face meeting. During the termination meeting, with the employee's manager and sometimes with a member of HR, the employee's building and systems access is deactivated, while the employee's co-workers are gathered together in a conference room. This allows the terminated employee a few minutes of privacy to gather personal belongings under the supervision of building security, HR, or the employee's manager. Then the terminated employee is escorted out of the building.

In some situations, terminated employees are given formal contracts known as separation agreements. The agreements state that the terminated employees agree not to sue the employer in exchange for some previously agreed-upon severance pay and/or other conditions.

Off-Boarding or Termination Activities

When an employee exits an organization, it is important to have a clear set of steps and actions outlined to ensure that all areas are addressed. Off-boarding activities vary, depending on the type of termination. Employees who are voluntarily resigning or retiring have a different exit process from employees being terminated for inappropriate behavior or policy violations. In general, though, there are many similar pieces of information that should be conveyed to an individual leaving an organization. These items could include:

- Turning in security badges and keys
- Turning in all equipment such as computers, phones, or other items
- Turning in uniforms and other company issued items such as credit cards
- Disabling access to internet and email systems
- Enabling "out of office" messages for email and phone
- Reviewing benefits information such as when health coverage will end, COBRA terms and conditions, retirement options, vacation and other leave payouts, and other items of importance
- Discussing the final paycheck, what it will include, and when it will be issued
- Ensuring accurate contact information including mailing address, email address, and phone numbers

A common best practice for employees exiting an organization is conducting an exit interview. Usually, these are best conducted with an individual who is voluntarily departing the organization. An **exit interview** is a conversation with a departing employee, in which an HR professional asks questions related to work experience, salary and benefits, training, concerns, and other topics that the organization wants to learn more about improving for the future. This is an excellent opportunity for the organization to find out what could be done better and what may have changed the employee's mind to stay with the organization.

There are also several activities that should be conducted by internal departments to ensure that business can continue as usual. If the exiting employee is a supervisor and responsible for managing employees, it is important to ensure that there is continuity for these employees in having a supervisor. Items such as approving leave requests, scheduling overtime, submitting and authorizing time cards, and handing out paychecks are all vital to the business operations. Ensuring there is a plan for handling these responsibilities is important to the organization and to the individual employees.

Finally, HR should announce the departure of the employee and the plan that will be implemented moving forward, especially if the termination is unexpected. Plans for moving forward could include redistributing the workload to other employees, recruiting a new employee to backfill the opening, or appointing an employee to fill the vacancy while plans are finalized. Losing an employee for any reason can have a huge impact to operations and other employees. Taking steps to coordinate the exit in a smooth and transparent manner can help reduce the potential of problems.

Employee Relations Programs

Employee Recognition

Employee recognition has been proven to be the most effective method of improving motivation and engaging employees. Regardless of the program, formality, award, or method, recognition is key to ensuring a high level of employee satisfaction and morale in an organization. Informal recognition programs can include the following:

- Recognizing a team or individual for a particular job well done in an employee newsletter
- Extending recognition during standing department meetings
- Saying thank you when an employee goes above and beyond
- Making sure employees feel appreciated in general

Formal recognition programs generally have a policy written to ensure that elements such as funding and budget, resources, and other specifics are identified. These programs can include the following:

- Service awards: 5 years, 10 years, 15 years
- Milestone service awards: 20 years, 25 years, 30 years
- Employee of the year
- Manager of the year

These awards may be given during a formal lunch, recognizing each individual and the contributions made to the organization. Gifts may be provided as well to truly convey a message of gratitude for the employee's hard work, dedication, and loyalty to the organization.

Employee Recognition Vendors

Due to a lack of staff resources, time, or in-house expertise, companies may choose to outsource their employee rewards program to a trusted recognition vendor. Since a vendor can, ultimately, determine the success or failure of a company's rewards program, there are a number of items that an employer should evaluate when entering into this type of relationship.

An exceptional recognition vendor will take the time to learn about a company's culture, business goals, employee rewards needs, and program budget. The recognition vendor should have an offering of high-quality awards and be able to accommodate rush orders and unique awards, if needed.

Additionally, world-class customer service is the key to employees receiving timely reward fulfillment and recognition for their efforts and achievements. An employer should be assured that the company will receive correct invoices and accurate reporting from the vendor. The ultimate goal for both the employer and the recognition vendor is to ensure that employees feel valued and remain loyal.

Special Events

Companies can use **special events** as a way to engage employees and promote a positive organizational culture. These events can involve managers serving lunch to employees during customer service appreciation week, organizing monthly employee events such as an ice cream social on a random Friday afternoon or an after-work happy hour, or planning an annual holiday party or company picnic for employees to enjoy with their co-workers and their families at a local amusement park. Additionally, these events can incorporate an element of community service, such as employees getting together to assist a local organization (an animal shelter or a food bank) during a "day of caring" event. Employee wellness can also be factored into these special events by scheduling yoga classes onsite for employees to participate in, or by providing monthly chair massages in a conference room at a reduced price for staff.

Promoting Outreach, Diversity, and Inclusion

A commitment to diversity and inclusion improves a company's relationship with its employees, customers and clients, and the community. Both a business case and a legal case can be made for engaging in diversity and inclusion initiatives. As previously discussed, the EEOC prohibits discriminatory hiring practices. Companies may also be subject to affirmative action laws in their states, and companies that have contracts with the federal government must comply with several federal laws. Section 503 of the Rehabilitation Act of 1973, which applies to contractors with contracts over $10,000, requires those employers to take affirmative action for qualified individuals with disabilities. The Vietnam Era Veterans' Readjustment Assistance Act of 1974 (VEVRAA), later amended by the Jobs for Veterans Act, requires companies to have an affirmative action for veterans with service-connected disabilities and applies to contractors with 50 or more employees and contracts of $100,000 or over. Executive Order 11246 requires contractors with 50 or more employees and contracts of $50,000 or more to maintain an affirmative action program regarding women and minorities.

One common way for companies to improve community outreach and develop a new generation of diverse employees is through an internship program. Having interns can be a win-win for the company and the community. People who are new to their field have a chance to develop their skills and learn more about the business. The company gets to evaluate new talent and build a pool of prospective employees; many companies hire full-time employees from previous interns, and these employees already have a great deal of loyalty to and knowledge about the organization. However, federal law should still be considered when designing an internship program. The FLSA establishes clear guidelines regarding wages and overtime pay for employees; for-profit companies planning unpaid internship programs must ensure that their interns are not in fact employees, using a seven-point test created by the Department of Labor. Generally, the test evaluates whether unpaid interns are primarily gaining educational benefit, understand they will not be compensated, and are not displacing paid employees.

Organizations may also have employee resource groups (ERGs), which are formed by groups of employees who belong to similar demographic groups (for example, an ERG for female employees at a company, or one for veterans). ERGs help employees feel represented within the organization, allow them to build relationships and share experiences with others who can understand their background, and give employers valuable insights into the unique needs and perspectives of a specific employee group.

Workforce Reduction and Restructuring Terminology

Workforce Reduction (Downsizing)

Workforce reductions are the planned elimination of a number of personnel in order to make an organization more competitive.

Once a company realizes it has a talent surplus, Human Resources can take the following steps to implement a workforce reduction:

- Reduce employees' hours
- Implement a hiring freeze
- Institute a voluntary separation program, also known as an early retirement buyout program

Although workforce reductions help companies cut costs in the short term, they often hurt productivity. For an organization to successfully implement a workforce reduction, it should communicate with employees throughout the entire process, and provide downsized employees with outplacement services to assist with resume writing, career counseling, and interview preparation. It can also provide referral assistance to exiting employees. Companies should strive to build the trust and commitment of the remaining employees so as to boost employee morale, especially during a downsizing situation.

Employees who are laid off are typically asked to sign a document known as a **separation agreement and general release**. This document, when signed, is a legally binding agreement that states the employee cannot sue or make any claims against the company in exchange for agreed upon severance benefits. Severance pay is not required by law, but most companies will pay employees who are laid off a set number of weeks of salary continuation, based upon their years of service (typically one or two weeks' pay per year of service), to ease their financial burden and to preserve the organization's image. Some companies also include a continuation of healthcare benefits for a set period of time.

An employee is given the agreement during their exit meeting and is allowed to take it home and review it with a lawyer. They have twenty-one days to sign and return the agreement for an individual separation and forty-five days to sign and return the agreement in cases of a group reduction in force. Once the agreement is signed, an employee still has seven days to revoke their signature.

Mergers and Acquisitions (M&A)

Corporate restructuring that involves mergers and acquisitions require complying with certain laws and regulations and also performing due diligence to evaluate a business contract before making any big decisions. Due diligence is typically performed when a company is buying another company (acquisition) and helps to uncover any potential liabilities or evaluate business and financial risk.

The due diligence process may involve spending time at the business location, reviewing sales numbers, learning about future plans for expansion, and carefully studying documents with vendors such as purchase order and sales agreements. An attorney may be hired to assist with the due diligence process to check for any discrepancies and verify the validity of certain documents and contracts.

In order to cut costs, reduce inefficiencies, or recover financially from a recent downturn, a company may decide to dispose of some or all of its business units by selling the company to another company, closing down permanently, declaring bankruptcy, or relocating overseas (offshoring). This is known as divesting a business. **Divestitures** can help a company better manage its portfolio of assets by closing some units to focus on others, or by selling off one or more business units to recover from a loss.

Outplacement Practices

Outplacement practices are a best practice for dealing with outsourcing or reductions in force. Although severance packages are excellent tools that can include extensions of salary and benefits to assist with a transition out of an organization, it is also important to look at other options that can help employees with this difficult phase. Specialized services can include job search services with career counselors, resume writing workshops, training programs to develop new and in-demand skills, or even financial planning to deal with the loss of an income.

Although it is never possible to meet every need of every employee, organizations who make an attempt to provide additional support and resources during transition periods will see easier transitions. These smooth transitions can result in less disruption to services and to the remaining employees. It is also important to address the needs of the remaining employees; they are facing a difficult transition as well. Their work may be changing, their former colleagues are no longer in the workplace, and the work environment in general changes. It is important to be cognizant of these issues and provide support as needed to those remaining with the organization.

Alumni Program

Employee engagement can continue even after employees have left the organization. One way is through an alumni program that allows HR to communicate with and keep up with former employees. There are several reasons to maintain an alumni program. First, former employees can be a valuable source of referrals and rehires because they are already familiar with the structure, culture, and skills involved with the company. Former employees may also later become clients, customers, or consultants for the company. One way to ensure the effectiveness of such a program is to have a positive and professional process when employees leave the company. This ensures that former employees leave with a great impression of their former company, allowing them to act as ambassadors and relationship builders for the company even as they continue their careers elsewhere. Learning about an employee's future goals and securing their contact information before they leave sets the stage for future ongoing communication, which is also imperative. Personalized outreach messages—for example, information about entry-level positions for former interns versus consultancy opportunities for former specialists—ensure that communications are relevant and effective. Ways to evaluate the effectiveness of the company's alumni program include analyzing the number of rehires and how long they stay with the company upon rehire; analyzing the number and value of business connections made through former employees; and tracking the number of hiring referrals from former employees.

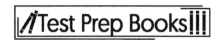

Practice Questions

1. Which of the following statements is true about the Landrum-Griffith Act?
   a. This act outlawed yellow-dog contracts.
   b. This act established the Federal Mediation and Conciliation Service.
   c. This act created the NLRB to encourage union growth.
   d. This act created a Bill of Rights for union members.

2. Which of the following pieces of legislation dictates what are known as unfair labor practices?
   a. The Wagner Act
   b. The Norris-LaGuardia Act
   c. The Taft-Hartley Act
   d. The Railway Labor Act

3. Which of the following is prohibited by the Taft-Hartley Act?
   a. The formation of monopolies
   b. Forcing employees to join a union
   c. Refusing to allow for a closed shop exception for construction trades
   d. Union members' inability to sue their union

4. Under the WARN Act, which of the following employers are required to provide a minimum of sixty days' notice to their employees in advance of a plant closing or mass layoff?
   a. An employer shuts down a plant facility that employs fifty total employees, twenty-five of which are working part-time. The company employs over one hundred full-time employees.
   b. Thirty full-time employees are laid off by a company at a single site that employs 120 full-time individuals for a three-month period.
   c. A company lays off 250 full-time employees at a single site that employs 650 full-time individuals for more than a six-month period.
   d. An employer shuts down a plant facility that has already been partially idled for quite some time. Only forty employees remain working at the site. The company employs over one hundred full-time employees.

5. Which of the following pieces of legislation established a commission to study how women and minorities face significant barriers and are prevented from reaching management positions?
   a. Title II
   b. The Civil Rights Act of 1991
   c. Equal Pay Act
   d. The Glass Ceiling Act

6. Which of the following is a guideline that focuses on organizational actions?
   a. Policy
   b. Rule
   c. Procedure
   d. Standard Operating Procedure (SOP)

7. Which of the following is more specific to the situation and is used to regulate and/or restrict an individual's behavior?
   a. Policy
   b. Rule
   c. Procedure
   d. Standard Operating Procedure (SOP)

8. In an organization with a progressive discipline policy, an employee has received a verbal warning for a performance issue. The same employee is later found to be in violation of a different company policy. How should this infraction be handled?
   a. The employee should be immediately terminated.
   b. The employee should receive coaching from their manager.
   c. The employee should receive a second warning, followed by a formal written warning.
   d. The employee should receive another verbal warning, since this is for a different violation.

9. After a staff member violates a work rule that is a dischargeable offense, an HR professional should follow through with which of the following actions?
   a. Terminate the staff member on the spot.
   b. Coach the staff member immediately.
   c. Give the staff member a final written warning.
   d. Conduct an investigation after placing the staff member on administrative leave.

10. The best guidelines for employee handbooks include which of the following?
   a. A disclaimer that states the handbook is not intended to be any type of contractual agreement between the company and employee.
   b. Requiring employees to sign off on revised versions of the handbook.
   c. Inclusion of policies that prevents the employee from leaving the company.
   d. Distributing printed copies of the handbook to new staff members during new employee orientation.

11. On January 1, 2015, an employer had 1,000 employees, and on December 31, 2015, the same employer had 1,200 employees. During the year, the employer had 125 employees exit from the organization. What is the employer's turnover rate for 2015?
   a. 10.42%
   b. 11.36%
   c. 12.5%
   d. 62.5%

12. Which of the following communication strategies is used to establish a relationship where employees feel comfortable speaking directly with management about problems and suggestions?
   a. Town hall meetings
   b. Management by Walking Around (MBWA)
   c. Open-door policy
   d. Department meetings

13. Which of the following communication strategies is used to allow management to check on employee progress, inquire about potential issues, and gain other feedback without relying on employees to "make the first move"?
   a. Open-door policy
   b. Brown bag lunch program
   c. Town hall meetings
   d. Management by Walking Around (MBWA)

14. Which of the following involvement strategies allows staff to work together in a temporary fashion to focus on a specific problem?
   a. Task force
   b. Committee
   c. Employee participation group
   d. Employee-management committee

15. Which of the following communication types, while making it easy to distribute information to a large group of individuals very quickly, may also lead to "information overload"?
   a. Intranet
   b. Email
   c. Newsletter
   d. Word-of-mouth

16. Which of the following is an example of an employee recognition program?
   a. An end of year bonus
   b. A plaque given for fifteen years of service to the organization
   c. A thank you note and a gift card for a job well done
   d. A merit given during annual review time

17. Which of the following is an example of a wrongful discharge?
   a. An employee who shared company information with a competitor
   b. An employee who takes home office supplies to help with an in-home consulting business
   c. An employee who accepts a gift in excess of $50 from a single client
   d. An employee who took time off from work to serve on a jury

18. Which of the following is true regarding severance pay?
   a. Severance pay is not required by law.
   b. Receipt of severance pay guarantees a former employee will not file a lawsuit against the employer.
   c. Severance pay increases an employer's contributions to unemployment tax.
   d. Severance pay guarantees that an employee will receive other benefits such as the continuation of health care coverage or outplacement services.

19. An HR professional uncovers during an exit interview that an employee is leaving the organization because she was bullied by two of her co-workers. The employee chose not to file any type of complaint or talk with HR during the course of her employment. She simply wants to leave the company and move on. Now that the HR professional is aware of the bullying and has details of the employee's experiences, what should the next move be?

a. Terminate the identified co-workers who were performing the bullying.
b. Conduct a full investigation and take the matter seriously.
c. Comply with the exiting employee's wishes and ignore the matter.
d. Let the matter go, since the affected employee is exiting the organization.

20. A company is laying off 20 percent of its workforce. Which of the following must be afforded to the individuals whose positions are being eliminated and are presented with documents known as a separation agreement and general release?

a. They must sign and return the agreement during the meeting where they are presented with it.
b. They must be given severance pay in return for signing the agreement.
c. They must be given a period of forty-five days to sign and return the agreement, with a seven-day revocation period.
d. They must be given the advantage of having a lawyer review the agreement for which they will be reimbursed by the company.

6/20 X

70%

Answer Explanations

1. D: The Landrum-Griffith Act created a Bill of Rights for union members. The Norris-LaGuardia Act outlawed yellow-dog contracts, Choice *A*. The Taft-Hartley Act established the Federal Mediation and Conciliation Service, Choice *B*. Finally, the Wagner Act created the NLRB to encourage union growth, Choice *C*.

2. A: The Wagner Act dictates what are known as unfair labor practices. The Norris-LaGuardia Act, Choice *B*, outlawed yellow-dog contracts. The Taft-Hartley Act, Choice *C*, established the Federal Mediation and Conciliation Service. The Railway Labor Act, Choice *D*, resolves labor disputes by substituting bargaining, arbitration, and mediation for strikes.

3. B: Forcing employees to join a union is prohibited by the Taft-Hartley Act. The Sherman Antitrust Act prevents individuals and organizations from forming monopolies, Choice *A*. The Landrum-Griffith Act allowed for a closed shop exception for construction trades and gave union members the right to sue their union, Choices *C* and *D*.

4. C: In Choice *C*, the employer has one hundred or more full-time employees. The mass layoff is expected to last for at least six months, and at least 33 percent of the workforce at the employment site is being laid off. Under the WARN Act, an employer is required to provide a minimum of sixty days' notice to their employees in advance of a mass layoff, if the employer has one hundred or more full-time employees (or a total of full-time and part-time employees working 4,000 hours per week, not counting overtime, at all of their employment sites combined) and the layoff will result in an employment loss at a single site for either fifty or more full-time employees, if they make up at least 33 percent of the workforce at the employment site, or 500 or more full-time employees, and the layoff is for more than six months. Under the WARN Act, an employer is required to provide a minimum of sixty days' notice to their employees in advance of a plant closing if the employer has one hundred or more full-time employees (or a total of full-time and part-time employees working 4,000 hours per week, not counting overtime, at all of their employment sites combined) and the plant closing will result in the temporary or permanent shutdown of an entire site or one or more facilities or operating units within a single site that results in an employment loss during any thirty-day period of fifty or more full-time employees.

5. D: The Glass Ceiling Act established a commission to study how women and minorities face significant barriers and are prevented from reaching management positions. This act was part of Title II of the Civil Rights Act of 1991, Choices *A* and *B*. Choice *C*, Equal Pay Act, is a law that seeks to abolish the wage disparity based on sex.

6. A: A policy is a guideline that focuses on organizational actions. A rule, Choice *B*, is more specific to the situation and is used to regulate and/or restrict an individual's behavior. A procedure, Choice *C*, is a detailed description that answers when, what, who, and where. Finally, a Standard Operating Procedure (SOP), Choice *D*, is a written set of instructions that documents how to perform a routine activity.

7. B: A rule is more specific to the situation and is used to regulate and/or restrict an individual's behavior. A policy, Choice *A*, is a guideline that focuses on organizational actions. A procedure, Choice *C*, is a detailed description that answers when, what, who, and where. Finally, a Standard Operating Procedure (SOP), Choice *D*, is a written set of instructions that documents how to perform a routine activity.

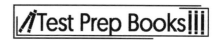

8. C: In a progressive discipline policy, a verbal warning is typically followed with a second warning that is paired with a formal written warning (even if the warning is for a different type of employee violation).

9. D: A staff member who violates a work rule that is a dischargeable offense does not need to go through all of the steps in the progressive discipline process before they are terminated. However, instead of terminating the staff member on the spot, it is best for an HR professional to place the staff member on administrative leave while conducting an investigation. This ensures that all parties are interviewed and all of the necessary facts are gathered to protect the company against any possible future claims of wrongful termination.

10. A: To guarantee that employment-at-will remains in effect, one of the best guidelines for employee handbooks is to include a disclaimer that states the handbook is not intended to be any type of contractual agreement between the company and employee.

11. B: The turnover rate is calculated by taking the number of employees that exited the company during the year, dividing it by the average number of employees during the year, and then multiplying that amount by 100. In this example, this equates to $\frac{125}{1100} \times 100$, which is 11.36%.

12. C: An open-door policy is used to establish a relationship where employees feel comfortable speaking directly with management about problems and suggestions. Town hall meetings, Choice A, formal gatherings for the entire company that are commonly referred to as "all-hands meetings," tend to focus on sharing information "from the top down" concerning the overall organization. These meetings are not usually designed to allow feedback from employees about smaller detail issues. Management by Walking Around (MBWA), Choice *B*, as the name suggests, involves having managers and supervisors physically get out of their offices and interact with employees in person. MBWA allows management to check on employee progress, inquire about potential issues, and gain other feedback without relying on employees to "make the first move." Finally, department meetings, Choice *D*, are formal gatherings of employees and management in a given department that typically take place on a set day and time, allow everyone involved to share ideas, and offer solutions to company challenges.

13. D: Management by Walking Around (MBWA), as the name suggests, involves having managers and supervisors physically get out of their offices and interact with employees in person. MBWA allows management to check on employee progress, inquire about potential issues, and gain other feedback without relying on employees to "make the first move." An open-door policy, Choice *A*, is used to establish a relationship where employees feel comfortable speaking directly with management about problems and suggestions. A brown bag lunch program, Choice *B*, is an informal meeting (usually including employees and management) that is used to discuss company problems over a "brown bag" lunch. The lunch setting and company-provided meal can help create a relaxed setting for exchanging ideas. Finally, town hall meetings, Choice *C*, tend to focus on sharing information "from the top down" concerning the overall organization. These meetings are not usually designed to allow feedback from employees about smaller detail issues.

14. A: A task force is an involvement strategy that allows staff to work together in a temporary fashion to focus on a specific problem. Employees can also work together in a formal capacity as part of a committee to address company concerns, Choice *B*. Committees may be temporary or ongoing, and employees' service on a committee may also be for a specific term or a permanent appointment. Moreover, an employee-management committee, Choice *D*, is a specific kind of committee where employees work alongside management to address company concerns. Sometimes known as employee participation groups, Choice C, these committees also can be temporary or ongoing, depending on the needs of the organization.

15. B: Email makes it easy to get information to a lot of people very quickly. However, this communication method can result in employees suffering from "information overload" from too many emails. The intranet, Choice *A*, has the benefit of no risk of important information being accessed by someone outside the organization. Intranets can be effective at communicating important ongoing information about the company, such as policies and procedures. Newsletters, Choice *C*, can provide a variety of information and have the potential to do so in an engaging and welcoming manner. However, newsletters can be labor-intensive. Finally, word-of-mouth, Choice *D*, can quickly spread information throughout a group of people. However, information can become muddled, misinterpreted, and unrecognizable as it is passed from person to person.

16. C: A thank you note and a gift card for a job well done is an example of an employee recognition program. An end of year bonus, Choice *A*, is an example of additional compensation an employee receives as a one-time payment that does not become part of their base pay. A plaque given for fifteen years of service to the organization, Choice *B*, is an example of a service award. Finally, a merit given during annual review time, Choice *D*, is an example of incentive pay given to employees for good performance.

17. D: Wrongful discharge can occur when an employee is terminated after they refuse to do something unsafe, unethical, or illegal, such as a pharmacist refusing to sign off on a prescription to be dispensed that does not have a date. This type of termination is wrongful because it violates public policy. Additionally, a charge of wrongful discharge can also occur when an employee is terminated after an employer promised them job security, thus violating an implied employment agreement. In this example, an employee should not be fired for taking time off work to serve on a jury, which falls under the category of violating public policy.

18. A: Severance pay is not required by law. Receipt of severance pay does not guarantee that a former employee will not file a lawsuit against the employer, Choice *B*. Severance pay does not increase an employer's contributions to unemployment tax, Choice *C*. Finally, severance pay does not guarantee that an employee will receive other benefits such as the continuation of health care coverage or outplacement services, Choice *D*.

19. B: Although the employee who was bullied is leaving the organization and did not file a complaint regarding the bullying during the course of her employment, the HR professional is still obligated to treat this matter seriously and should conduct a full investigation.

20. C: During a larger group RIF, the affected employees who are being laid off and given a document to sign, known as a separation agreement and general release, must be given forty-five days to sign and return the agreement, along with a seven-day revocation period. This allows them time to consider the terms of the agreement and to review the agreement with a lawyer, if they choose to do so.

Health, Safety, and Security

Laws and Regulations Related to Workplace Health, Safety, Security, and Privacy

Workplace policies should strictly follow federal laws in order to legally secure a workplace that satisfies minimum health, safety, security, and privacy standards. Failure to meet federal standards can result in fines or the loss of a license. Federal laws and regulations function as minimum standards that all workplace policies must meet. Employers are allowed to pursue policies that go beyond what is legally required if they believe such policies will benefit the organization. Many employers strive to understand the delicate balance between meeting federal guidelines and maintaining high profit margins. Therefore, organizations often find innovative ways to meet federal standards while using efficient business strategies.

Five federal agencies and laws regarding workplace issues are the Occupational Safety and Health Administration (OSHA), the Drug-Free Work Place Act, the Americans with Disabilities Act, the Health Insurance Portability and Accountability Act, and the Sarbanes-Oxley Act.

The **Occupational Safety and Health Act** (**OSHA**) regulations focus on employer and employee rights and responsibilities. Employers must provide a safe workplace for employees. Employers are required to meet all OSHA safety standards and correct any violations. Employers are required to attempt to reduce hazards to workers and must supply free protective equipment to workers. OSHA guidelines require employers to provide safety training and to prominently display OSHA posters that detail employee rights. Employers must keep accurate records of any injuries or illnesses that occur in the workplace and notify OSHA promptly of any injuries. Furthermore, employers may not retaliate if an employee uses their right to report an OSHA violation.

OSHA regulations provide specific rights to employees. Employees have the right to demand safety on the job and obtain information concerning work hazards. Every employee has the right to file a complaint with OSHA and request a workplace inspection without fear of employer retaliation. Employees have the right to meet privately with a licensed OSHA inspector. Additionally, OSHA regulations allow employees to refuse work that may be abnormally dangerous or life-threatening.

The **Drug-Free Workplace Act of 1988** requires organizations to establish a drug-free workplace, provide a copy of this policy to their employees, and institute a drug awareness program. This law applies to federal contractors with contracts of $100,000 or more and all organizations that are federal grantees. Different penalties exist for employers who do not comply with the act, including contract suspension or contract termination. Although an employer may discuss alcohol and tobacco use in its policies, the Drug-Free Workplace Act does not address the use of these substances.

The **Americans with Disabilities Act** (**ADA**) is a federal law that prevents discrimination based on disability. This law requires employers to provide reasonable accommodations to employees with a disability. For example, an employer may accommodate a disabled employee by building a wheelchair accessible ramp to enter and exit the building. Additionally, the ADA stipulates that public entities be accessible for disabled persons. The ADA does include both mental and physical medical conditions, and temporary conditions may qualify as a disability. ADA protections apply to every aspect of job application procedures, employment, and promotions.

The **Health Insurance Portability and Accountability Act of 1996 (HIPAA)** addresses issues of healthcare access and portability as well as aspects of healthcare administration. HIPAA provisions allow workers that change jobs or become unemployed to transfer and continue their healthcare coverage. Additionally, HIPAA regulations establish standards for healthcare administration in order to reduce waste, fraud, and abuse. HIPAA laws strengthen privacy standards and provide benchmarks for medical records in areas such as electronic billing.

HIPAA is applicable to health insurance plans issued by companies, HMOs, Medicare, and Medicaid. Moreover, these regulations apply to healthcare providers who conduct transactions electronically and healthcare clearing houses that process certain information. HIPAA's Privacy Rule gives rights to the insured regarding the disclosure of medical information. Individuals may view health records and request an edit of inaccurate information. Additionally, individuals may file a complaint if rights are being denied or health information is not protected. Patient information with heightened protection is placed in the insurer's database and may include conversations about patients between medical professionals and billing information. Lastly, HIPAA creates strict rules regarding how healthcare information is disseminated and specifies who is given access.

The **Sarbanes-Oxley Act of 2002**, or **SOX**, is federal legislation that is designed to establish higher levels of accountability and standards for U.S. public institution boards and senior management. The act was passed in reaction to major global corporate and accounting scandals such as WorldCom and Enron, companies caught engaging in dubious financial practices. Sarbanes-Oxley specifically targets senior executives responsible for accounting misconduct and record manipulation. The law protects shareholders from any activity that conceals or misleads investors about the firm's finances. The firm has a mandate to transparently and accurately report financial information either to shareholders or the Securities and Exchange Commission (SEC). Moreover, SOX imposes more stringent penalties for white-collar crime and requires detailed reporting to the SEC if a company's finances significantly alter.

Risk Mitigation in the Workplace

Protecting employees, minimizing loss, and developing effective safety procedures are central goals for a successful organization. In order to meet these goals, firms must establish robust and creative policies, procedures, and standards.

Lawsuits

Employers should protect themselves from the risk of lawsuits by complying with all applicable state, federal, and local labor laws. Knowledge of labor laws is not specifically the purview of Human Resources (HR), either; HR leaders should ensure that leaders throughout the organization are familiar with key regulations. This can be achieved through communication initiatives such as training sessions or posting notices about labor regulations as required by law. There are many laws protecting workers' rights. The Occupational Safety and Health Administration (OSHA) oversees and enforces workplace safety regulations. One such regulation is the Hazard Communication Standard, which includes standards for safety measures such as the labeling of workplace hazards. Title VIII of the Sarbanes-Oxley Act of 2002 (also known as Sarbox or SOX) provides protections for corporate whistleblowers and describes the penalties for interfering with fraud investigations. Title I of the Americans with Disabilities Act (ADA) applies to employers with fifteen or more employees and outlines legal protections for qualified employees with disabilities, including their legal right to reasonable accommodation in the workplace as long as it does not place an undue hardship on the employer.

Emergency Response

All organizations must have procedures that secure an orderly response in the event of an emergency. Emergency response plans incorporate several elements of maintaining safety and order. These elements may include practiced evacuations, reserved resources to preserve organizational function, and a plan that seeks to minimize property damage. An organization with no emergency response plan is vulnerable to instability, disorder, and distrust. An effective emergency response plan not only protects lives and property but provides security that management has control over the situation. This knowledge provides an element of calm in an otherwise stressful emergency situation, which can be as important as the response protocol.

An **emergency response** is planned, and practiced protocol is used during an emergency. These strategies should be planned rationally and practiced frequently in order to mitigate the impact of a disaster. Workplace emergency responses should plan for a wide range of scenarios, such as machinery malfunctions or workplace violence. Once created, emergency response plans should be communicated to all staff, frequently tested by the organization, and kept up to date.

An **evacuation** is a coordinated and planned exit from a place that is considered to be dangerous. It is a principal component of general health and safety policies. Conditions that may prompt evacuation are fire, flood, or violence. The most effective way to orchestrate an orderly and calm evacuation is through practice of an evacuation plan. This routine practice familiarizes staff with expedient exit routes and ensures that exits remain visible and unobstructed.

Hazard communication is the notification of employees concerning the noxious health effects and physical dangers of hazardous chemicals in the workplace. Workers should be clearly notified of any physical hazards (corrosion or flammability) or health hazards (skin irritation and carcinogenicity) that they will come into contact with in the workplace. OSHA created the **Hazard Communication Standard** (**HCS**) to ensure that chemical information is accessible to all individuals who may interact with the substance. In addition to the HCS, all employers are required to implement a hazard communication program that encompasses training, access to material safety data sheets (MSDS), and labeling of hazardous chemical containers.

Risk Management

An organization engages in risk management when it identifies, targets, and strives to minimize unacceptable risks. While a variety of different risks may arise, an organization's principal risks are generally workplace health, safety, security, and privacy. Failure to protect from these risks can result in serious consequences and may lead to negative company publicity, low employee morale, and burdensome expenses. Organizations must prioritize risk management and comply with federal laws and regulations. By doing so, employers will increase productivity and build sustainable relationships between employees and management.

Cost-Benefit Analysis (CBA)

A **cost-benefit analysis** (**CBA**) is an important factor in many business decisions. A CBA compares the cost of a particular option with the benefits it will bring to the organization. A CBA has two main uses. First, it helps to determine whether a particular option is worthwhile (Do the benefits sufficiently offset the costs?). Secondly, it's a method of comparison when making a decision that has several options.

Of course, any cost-benefit analysis involves a certain level of uncertainty because it's predicting future values under future conditions. For example, a change in the cost of a certain resource or the exchange rate of foreign currency could impact the results of a CBA. For this reason, a CBA usually includes a sensitivity analysis, which determines how much a change in uncertain variables will affect the CBA. This sensitivity analysis takes into account the expected conditions (what will happen if everything proceeds according to the status quo?) as well as worst-case conditions (what will happen if all possible problems arise in this situation?). In this way, a CBA can also reveal the level of risk involved in a decision. An option that appears attractive at first may seem less certain after a sensitivity analysis.

A cost-benefit analysis can also be approached differently depending on the view of the analysis—short-, mid-, or long-term. For many business decisions, the costs are upfront while the benefits may appear immediately or after a longer period of time. For this reason, a short-term and long-term CBA could yield very different results. If an organization needs a quick return on benefits, it might place more emphasis on a short-term CBA. However, if it's willing to wait longer to reap the benefits of a decision, it might compare its options based on long-term CBAs.

Enterprise Risk Management (ERM)

No matter how carefully an organization conducts research, carries out analyses, and develops strategic plans, the organization will always face unknowns. There are risks that activities will fail, outside obstacles will appear, or new threats will emerge. **Enterprise risk management** (**ERM**) is a method of managing unknowable risks by anticipating potential risks, focusing on those with the greatest likelihood or potential impact, and planning a response strategy for when risks become realities.

An organization could choose four different responses to a particular risk: reduce the effects of the risk, share it, avoid it, or accept it. In order to reduce the effects of the risk, the organization finds ways to decrease its likelihood or to soften its potential harmful impact. If the organization wants to avoid the risk altogether, it will simply cease all activity associated with that risk. Finally, an organization might decide to go ahead and accept a risk; this might happen when cost-benefit analysis has determined that the benefits greatly outweigh all potential risk to the organization.

Risk management is especially important in human resources, which can account for a significant portion of an organization's financial risk, especially in terms of liability and legal concerns. For example, the organization can be held liable for compliance (or non-compliance) with labor laws, proper management of employee information, and legal concerns of employees like workplace safety and sexual harassment. HR can identify which risks are the most pressing for their organization and plan accordingly, perhaps through an HR audit. Like any audit, an HR audit is an inspection—in this case, of an organization's HR policies and practices. The purpose of an HR audit is to check that policies are in line with all applicable laws and regulations and are properly followed by all employees.

Workplace Violence Conditions

Workplace violence is any act of physical violence, intimidation, threat, or verbal abuse that occurs in the workplace. This behavior is disruptive both physically and psychologically. Employees may demonstrate violent behavior as a result of a history of violence, a troubled upbringing, issues of substance abuse, and psychological illness. These conditions may foster violent behavior from an employee but do not make violent behavior inevitable. Workplace violence not only interrupts immediate employees, but can cause an organization to lose clients, suppliers, and advertisers. Furthermore, a firm can suffer devastating economic consequences as a result of negative publicity from incidents of workplace violence. Workplace violence attacks the foundation of trust and safety that all workplaces need to operate successfully.

Although an employer cannot completely eliminate the possibility of workplace violence, several steps can be taken to avoid these incidents. One example is a mental health program, such as an Employee

Assistance Program (EAP), which provides employees the option to improve their psychological wellbeing. Additionally, offering company parties and functions in alcohol-free locations may reduce the likeliness of workplace violence. Violence may also be introduced in the workplace from the public. In areas with high crime rates, statistics show a higher probability of violence for employers who operate at night. Finally, organizations should establish and enforce a zero-tolerance policy for on-site weapons and acts of violence.

Workplace Safety Risks

Minimizing injuries in the workplace is a primary concern for employers. Accidents and injuries triggered by safety risks diminish productivity and reduce savings because of costly workers' compensation payments. Furthermore, failure to adequately protect workers can result in employer penalties and fines. Two common workplace safety risks are tripping hazards and blood-borne pathogens.

Trip hazards cause a person's foot to hit an object that does not budge, plunging the person forward involuntarily. Tripping can occur in the workplace for many reasons such as obstructed views, poor lighting, excessive clutter, uneven walking surfaces, wrinkled carpeting, or unsecure wires. Tripping may result in injuries such as sprains, broken bones, or torn ligaments. Employers should maintain an orderly workplace and arrange for bright lighting to reduce the likelihood of tripping. Accordingly, employees should pay attention when walking, make wide turns when walking, and walk with feet pointed outward.

Bloodborne pathogens are infectious microorganisms in human blood that can cause disease in humans. Specifically, some of these pathogens are hepatitis B virus (HBV), hepatitis C virus (HCV), and human immunodeficiency virus (HIV). One potential cause of spreading bloodborne pathogens is through improper usage and/or disposal of needles. Occupations such as nursing, healthcare professionals, medical first responders, and housekeepers who work in medical environments are the most likely to encounter a needle with bloodborne pathogens. Due to growing concerns within the medical field, The Needlestick Safety and Prevention Act of 2000 revised OSHA's Bloodborne Pathogens Standard. This law provides requirements in selecting medical devices and establishes oversight through a sharps' injury log, which details all sharps-related workplace injuries.

Additional workplace safety risks with OSHA regulations are occupational noise exposure, emergency exit procedures, control of hazardous materials, lockout/tagout procedures, machine guarding, and confined space environments.

Workers' compensation laws are designed to protect employees who are injured in the workplace. The primary purpose of workers' compensation is to provide injured employees with fixed monetary sums. Workers' compensation benefits cover medical expenses due to workplace injuries. Furthermore, workers' compensation benefits are extended to dependents of employees killed by an injury or illness that occurs in the workplace. In addition to employee protection, some workers' compensation laws protect employers by limiting the amount of money that can be distributed to employees. The program also has provisions that restrict co-worker liability in most workplace accidents. Most workers' compensation programs are structured at the state level by legislative bodies and agencies. However, worker's compensation exists at the federal level, where it is limited to federal employment and industries that considerably affect interstate commerce.

Security Risks in the Workplace

Security Plans

Obtaining a safe and secure working environment is not accomplished by simply strategizing. The staff of an organization must have adequate training to appropriately respond to diverse situations. Workplace security plans and policies address a variety of issues from a sudden crisis to an act of intentional harm. A clear understanding of security plans and policies can minimize unpredictability and panic and teach employees how to respond to a crisis.

Employees should understand security plans and how they address the physical security needs of the work environment. Workplace security plans and policies may include security measures such as control badges, keycard access systems, backup communication systems, locks on various rooms and closets, and concealed alarms. When developing workplace security plans, a team approach is vital to ensuring its success. Representatives are needed from human resources, legal counsel, security, and facilities to provide a comprehensive perspective of security needs. Once the security plans and policies are established, employees should be trained annually to review the plans and their importance.

Theft

Theft is the act of taking property without the consent of the owner. Theft can occur by deception or force, with or without the knowledge of the owner. Theft can be very costly to an organization, and management should take steps to prevent any opportunity for theft. Such measures may include hidden video cameras, a private security force, and incentives for employees who disrupt incidents of theft. Theft can be accomplished by employees, management, and customers. Therefore, prevention policies should apply to all levels of the organization.

Corporate Espionage

Corporate espionage is a form of spying that occurs between competitive companies. The principal purpose of corporate espionage is to obtain industrial secrets and learn about a competitor's plans, future products, business strategies, or total profits. Knowing these secrets can give a competitor an unfair advantage when trying to increase market share. A company must hire trustworthy employees, particularly employees privy to classified information. A firm should employ strategies to test employee loyalty and offer incentives that encourage employees to report suspicious activity.

Sabotage

Sabotage is the act of purposely weakening or corrupting a country or a company. In the workplace, sabotage is the intentional thwarting of successful planning models to create dysfunctional conditions at odds with the organization's best interests. Those who commit sabotage are known as saboteurs, and they generally conceal their identity and intentions. Sabotage is debilitating to a company and can cultivate an environment of distrust and hostility. Therefore, management must conduct frequent tests to ensure that all members and employees act in good faith.

Practice Questions

1. What was the principal intent of the Sarbanes-Oxley Act of 2002 (SOX)?
   a. The SOX Act deregulated accounting standards for senior executives of accounting firms.
   b. The SOX Act established high levels of transparency and accountability for senior executives in accounting and recordkeeping.
   c. The SOX Act encouraged companies to increase transparency for shareholders by offering subsidies for compliance.
   d. The SOX Act decreased protections for shareholders that were defrauded by institutions.

2. Which is a true statement about the Americans with Disabilities Act (ADA)?
   a. The ADA is a federal law that prevents discrimination based on disability and requires employers to provide reasonable accommodations to disabled employees.
   b. The ADA applies only to full-time employees, but not part-time or temporary employees.
   c. The ADA exempts private employers and only applies to municipal, state, and federal organizations.
   d. The ADA was included in the Civil Rights Act of 1964.

3. What is a true statement about alternative work locations?
   a. No companies have experimented with alternative work locations, so their benefits cannot yet be evaluated.
   b. Alternative work locations are generally discouraged since it is difficult to trust employees to work outside of the office.
   c. Alternative work locations have been proven to reduce employee productivity.
   d. Because alternative work locations help decentralize operations, the organization is better protected from the destructive efforts of a single person.

4. Why should employers train employees to use social media effectively?
   a. Employers generally do not like to train employees to use social media because it can be a distraction from their work.
   b. An employee with social media skills provides an organization with an advantage in the fields of marketing and advertising.
   c. Employees using social media are friendlier in the work environment.
   d. If employees can use social media, they are more likely to be up to date on current news.

5. Does OSHA offer any rights to employees, and if so, what do these rights entail?
   a. OSHA does not offer rights to employees, only safety protections.
   b. OSHA does grant rights to employees, such as the right to a pay increase if hazardous substances are introduced to the workplace.
   c. OSHA does grant rights to employees, such as the right to register complaints against their employer without fear of retaliation and the right to meet privately with an OSHA inspector.
   d. OSHA does grant rights to employees, but only after one year of employment.

6. What is a needs analysis?

a. A needs analysis is a data-gathering activity where all members of an organization are surveyed about specific needs and requests. This information is assessed and then employed in ways to improve the functionality of the organization.

b. A needs analysis is a data-gathering activity where only senior management is surveyed about their specific needs and requests. This information is assessed and then employed in ways to improve the functionality of the organization.

c. A needs analysis is a data-gathering activity where all members of an organization are surveyed about specific needs and requests. However, the surveys must be completed in secret because employees can be fired for expressing critical views of management.

d. A needs analysis is a data-gathering activity only performed at a company after a major safety or security incident.

Answer Explanations

1. B: The Sarbanes-Oxley Act (SOX) established high levels of transparency and accountability for senior executives in accounting and recordkeeping. Passed in the wake of global corporate accounting scandals, SOX provides greater protection to shareholders and investors by emphasizing transparency and accountability. The legislation mandates that senior executives report financial information to shareholders and the Securities and Exchange Committee (SEC). Furthermore, SOX imposes harsher penalties for white-collar crime and requires detailed reporting to the SEC whenever there is a significant fluctuation in a company's finances.

2. A: The Americans with Disabilities Act (ADA) is a federal law that prevents discrimination based on disability and requires employers to provide reasonable accommodations to disabled employees. Additionally, the ADA stipulates that public entities be accessible for disabled persons. The law applies to all types of work (part-time, full-time, or work during a temporary period) in organizations with fifteen or more employees. The ADA became a law in 1990.

3. D: Alternative work locations permit organizations to decentralize operations, thus minimizing the possibility for a person to cause significant destruction.

4. B: Employees who possess an aptitude for social media skills provide an additional asset to the company in the areas of marketing and advertising.

5. C: OSHA provides specific rights to workers. These rights include the right to register complaints against their employer without fear of retaliation and the right to meet privately with an OSHA inspector. Lastly, OSHA guidelines give workers the right to receive any information pertaining to health risks and hazards on the job.

6. A: A needs analysis is the process in which an organization gathers information about the principal needs and requests of its members. This analysis studies the expectations and requirements of subjects who are affected by workplace programs or regulations. Surveys and questionnaires are the primary means of procuring information about specific needs and requests. After the needs analysis is conducted, the information is assessed and incorporated into plans to improve the functionality of the organization.

Dear aPHR Test Taker,

We would like to start by thanking you for purchasing this study guide for your aPHR exam. We hope that we exceeded your expectations.

Our goal in creating this study guide was to cover all of the topics that you will see on the test. We also strove to make our practice questions as similar as possible to what you will encounter on test day. With that being said, if you found something that you feel was not up to your standards, please send us an email and let us know.

We have study guides in a wide variety of fields. If you're interested in one, try searching for it on Amazon or send us an email.

Thanks Again and Happy Testing!
Product Development Team
info@studyguideteam.com

FREE Test Taking Tips DVD Offer

To help us better serve you, we have developed a Test Taking Tips DVD that we would like to give you for FREE. **This DVD covers world-class test taking tips that you can use to be even more successful when you are taking your test.**

All that we ask is that you email us your feedback about your study guide. Please let us know what you thought about it – whether that is good, bad or indifferent.

To get your **FREE Test Taking Tips DVD**, email freedvd@studyguideteam.com with "FREE DVD" in the subject line and the following information in the body of the email:

a. The title of your study guide.

b. Your product rating on a scale of 1-5, with 5 being the highest rating.

c. Your feedback about the study guide. What did you think of it?

d. Your full name and shipping address to send your free DVD.

If you have any questions or concerns, please don't hesitate to contact us at freedvd@studyguideteam.com.

Thanks again!

Made in the USA
Columbia, SC
02 February 2021